DATE DUE			
DEC 2 '70			
FEB 3 '71			
MAR 17 '71			
4-21-71			
4/27/71			
MAR 22			
MAR 22 '72			

GAYLORD M-2   PRINTED IN U.S.A.

COLD WAR DIPLOMACY

American Foreign Policy, 1945–1960

NORMAN A. GRAEBNER

Professor of History
University of Illinois

AN ANVIL ORIGINAL

under the general editorship of

LOUIS L. SNYDER

D. VAN NOSTRAND COMPANY, INC.

PRINCETON, NEW JERSEY

TORONTO   LONDON

This book is dedicated to George F. Kennan
in recognition of his contribution to the
study of American foreign policy

VAN NOSTRAND REGIONAL OFFICES:
New York, Chicago, San Francisco

D. VAN NOSTRAND COMPANY, LTD., *London*

D. VAN NOSTRAND COMPANY (Canada), LTD., *Toronto*

Published simultaneously in Canada by
D. VAN NOSTRAND COMPANY (Canada), LTD.

PRINTED IN THE UNITED STATES OF AMERICA

TABLE OF CONTENTS

COLD WAR DIPLOMACY
American Foreign Policy, 1945–1960

Part I

AMERICAN FOREIGN POLICY, 1945-1960

— 1 —

INTRODUCTION: THE ISOLATIONIST TRADITION

For the American people the fifteen years from 1945 to 1960 comprised an original experience. Never before in a time of comparative peace were they so fully involved in world affairs. As the guardians of Western civilization they had little choice, for that civilization had entered upon troubled times. Tragically the suicidal tendencies within Western Europe, characterized largely by that region's inability to integrate the German Empire into its political structure, had the effect of propelling two great powers to the forefront of world politics. That the United States and Russia in 1945 would face one another across a weak and demoralized Europe was predicted by the mere act of crushing the might of Germany. But this apparent military necessity in itself presaged no unique or permanent American involvement in affairs beyond its own shores. Most Americans assumed, indeed, that with the establishment of peace the two great Allies, through their cooperation and mutual support of the decisions of the United Nations, would guarantee at last the creation of a new world order based on law and justice. Beyond victory lay a world not unlike that of the inter-war years with the traditional balance of power—always the chief source of American security—firmly re-established in Europe.

What perpetuated the nation's traditional illusion of isolation, even at a time of total involvement, was the fact that the war always remained far from its own shores. Since German power, once disposed of by an Allied victory, entailed no continuing infringement on Western security, the United States really had no political or military interest in Europe other than that of imposing some restrictions on the defeated nations. Nothing in the war itself challenged the American isolationist tradition.

Only the most astute observers during the war could see that the United States, in its pursuit of total victory, was helping to create a new balance of power that would prove to be as unacceptable as that created by Hitler. Any return to normalcy required a Russian withdrawal to its prewar boundaries and, in general, its prewar status in world affairs—to be achieved quite automatically through the Soviet acceptance of the principle of self-determination of peoples. Fundamentally, the Atlantic Charter promised a postwar world without permanent victors or permanent losers. For the American people, having suffered no invasion, this was both a feasible and a moral arrangement.

But Russian vulnerability to penetration from the west, demonstrated again in the recent experience of war, prompted the Kremlin to seek some tangible evidence of victory. Unfortunately, the Soviets could not impose their will on regions subject to their armies without both defying their wartime commitments to self-determination and raising doubts regarding their ultimate intentions. It was not certain that the U.S.S.R., having broken one set of promises, would not continue its westward course as subsequent opportunities presented themselves. When American leadership in 1947 became convinced that the Soviet Union represented an expansive rather than a stabilizing force in European politics, it wrote its fears into the nation's economic and military containment policies. But even these momentous decisions comprised no sharp break with the nation's traditional distaste for power politics. As in its previous twentieth-century involvements in European affairs, the United States quickly identified its military and diplomatic entanglements with a new crusade for freedom.

This deepening commitment to the safety of Western Europe and the increasing emphasis on military preparedness created the notion that the United States had at last entered upon a career not unlike those of the great powers of the past. This was not true. If the United States, because of its wealth and power, had a continuing impact on events throughout the world, its policies had far more in common with the Wilsonism and isolationism of the interwar years than with the *realpolitik* of a Richelieu, Canning, or Bismarck. For what distinguished the statesmanship of such men was not the wielding of massive power or the inclination to interfere but the accurate and painstaking definition of their nations' interests in terms of available power and the interests of others. Not since the nineteenth century had the United States analyzed its needs in such concrete terms. Between the wars the inclination of American leadership to embrace the cause of humanity permitted it to come to grips with nothing.

This tendency to pursue abstractions rather than concrete interests continued to dominate American diplomacy in the postwar era. The central fact in the country's response to the Soviet challenge was the absence of any clearly-defined body of objectives that had some relationship to American capability or even genuine intention. If future historians, examining these troubled years, could credit the United States with a truly beneficial role in world affairs, it would be not because this nation held within its grasp an unprecedented capacity to destroy or because it was adept at verbalizing utopias for itself, neither of which required much imagination, but because it recognized its fundamental interests amid the varied challenges of the age and defended them with determination.

What gave consistency to the American outlook on the world from 1900 to 1960 was the essential fact that the United States entered the present century as a satiated power. For such a nation there is always an identity between its interest in stability and its appeal to abstract principles, for the application of democratic and legal processes to international affairs assures not only the continuance of peace and order but also the perpetuation of the established hierarchy of power. Were the United States an aggressive, imperialistic country, as it was during much of the nineteenth century, its diplomatic language would contain fewer references to principle. In large measure the postwar appeal to the concepts of the Atlantic Charter, like the prewar appeal to the sanctity of treaties, appeared to much of the globe as an inexpensive, if futile, effort of the United States to deflate its enemies. During the thirties the perennial refusal of the country to concede its principles and demand nothing less than their fulfillment forced American leadership to respond to the threats of German and Japanese aggression with little but words of disapprobation. After World War II this deeply-ingrained habit of over-demanding reduced much of the nation's action toward the Kremlin to a similar pattern of behavior, for nothing else remained.

It is tragic that this neglect of the fundamental obligation of government to maintain some relationship between ends and means in national action accustomed the American people to expect too much of foreign policy. Dean Rusk, as an able and experienced American diplomat, wrote several years ago:

> There are few fields of human endeavor where wishful thinking and self-delusion are as common, or as dangerous as in foreign policy. We demand simple answers to the most complex questions confronting human intelligence. We expect consistency in policy, though the facts themselves are full of contradictions. We should like an easy way to carry a heavy burden, an agreeable way to perform disagreeable tasks, a cheap way to bring about an expensive result.

Herein lay the traditional American dilemma. Whatever the energy or determination of its antagonists, the nation was always assured that it could anticipate the eventual collapse of its enemies and the creation of the illusive world of justice and freedom. Certainly all fundamental American relations with the U.S.S.R. and mainland China after 1950 were anchored to that assumption. What is dangerous in any such promise of victory at little or no cost is the failure of leadership to prepare the people either for peace or for war. It creates a vague and optimistic national detachment from external crises. What was so perilously true in the troubled days before Pearl Harbor was equally true in the fifties.

This nation's permanent involvement in world affairs made unprecedented demands upon its resources and its energies. Far less obvious, but far more disturbing, was the nation's perennial inability to divest itself of its isolationist habits of mind. It continued throughout the fifties to expect too much of its enemies and too little of itself under the unshakable assumption that its superior virtue somehow eliminated the need to pay the normal price of maintaining even its elementary interests in a world of conflict. The refusal of the United States to define its requirements in negotiable terms permitted it no escape, except that of war, from the diplomatic challenges of the thirties. Yet it learned so little from that experience that after 1945 it neglected again, in its appeal to principle, to define those areas of turmoil and conflict where its interests and its capabilities converged. In the long run a nation cannot escape its challenges. The substitution of words of disapprobation and other devices of drift for serious negotiation are at best a play for time beyond which the concrete issues in conflict must always be resolved either by diplomacy or by war.

2 —

THE NEW BALANCE OF POWER

For the American people in 1945 victory over the Axis was synonymous with utopia. The nation's giant crusade against "the makers of war, the breeders of hate," as President Franklin D. Roosevelt had termed the German leaders, had managed to assign all the world's evil to the enemy of the moment. Through crushing military force the peace-loving nations would disarm the criminals and adopt measures to prevent them from disturbing the peace again. Under Secretary of State Joseph C. Grew, in January, anchored his optimism for the future to the "upsurge of determination among the peoples of the world as has never before been seen in history—the determination that war, like slavery and disease, must go." Beyond the destruction of Germany and Japan, then, lay not a continuance of the struggle for power among nations, but a new era of international cooperation based on the principles of the Atlantic Charter.

This mood of assurance that the year would reap a harvest, not of victory alone, but of lasting peace, continued to mount throughout the spring of 1945. The apparent agreements of the Big Three at Yalta in February was evidence enough that the wartime unity of the great powers would continue into the postwar world. The American and Soviet acceptance of the United Nations Organization was merely the final guarantee that the search for world order would not fail. The reaffirmation of the principles agreed to at Dumbarton Oaks in the fall of 1944 demonstrated, in the words of *Time,* "that World War II was not being fought in vain." Senator Alben W. Barkley of Kentucky characterized the Yalta Conference "as one of the most important steps ever taken to promote peace and happiness in the world." The President confirmed the deep sense of achievement when he reported to a joint session of Congress on March 1 that "never before have the major Allies been more closely united— not only in their war aims but in their peace aims." The Crimean Conference, he added hopefully, "spells the end of the system of unilateral action and exclusive alliances and spheres of influence and balance of power and all the other expedients that have been tried for centuries—and have failed. We propose to substitute for all these a universal organization in which all peace-loving nations will finally have a chance to join."

Whatever doubts the national leadership harbored concerning Russia's postwar intentions were not conveyed to the American people. The U.S.S.R. had subscribed to the principle of self-determination of peoples as embodied in the Atlantic Charter. This action enrolled her in the legion of the good and appeared to assure her cooperation in the creation of the new utopia. The new President,

Harry S. Truman, gave public expression to his confidence in May on the occasion of VE Day: "United, the peace-loving nations have demonstrated in the West that their arms are stronger by far than the might of dictators or the tyranny of military cliques that once called us soft and weak." What the President failed to observed at that moment of triumph was that Russia was not necessarily peace-loving in the American sense, and that without her support the democracies would not have won at all. This was not a victory of democracy alone, but democracy supported by the world's greatest dictatorship, the Soviet Union.

The Allied Conflict Over Eastern Europe. Unfortunately, the well-established facts of international life scarcely warranted the Western expectation of a new world order based on the Wilsonian principles of justice and self-determination. Throughout the war it was clear that Allied interests coincided only on the issue of defeating the common enemy. The United States and Great Britain entered the war as satiated powers, seeking nothing but peace and stability in world affairs. They had written their moral and limited purpose into the Atlantic Charter as early as August, 1941. For the Kremlin this repudiation of the tangible and lasting emoluments of victory was never an acceptable basis of action. Whether Russia eventually signed the Atlantic Charter or not, she would not settle for a world based on the principle of self-determination. Any assumption that she would expected too much denial of that country's historic problems and ambitions.

At no time during the war did Stalin hide his intention of creating a new European order which would serve the interests of the Soviet Union. For centuries the rulers of Russia had viewed the disallowance of Poland and other areas of Eastern Europe to any antagonist as a matter of life and death. The ease with which the anti-Soviet governments of Slavic Europe fell into Nazi hands prompted Stalin in December, 1941, to demand of Anthony Eden that Britain recognize the "Curzon Line" as the new Soviet-Polish frontier as well as the transfer to Russia of certain Rumanian military facilities. To the American Secretary of State, Cordell Hull, it was unthinkable that Russia should gain any territorial concessions as the result of the war. He reminded Eden that the postwar policies of the United States

> have been delineated in the Atlantic Charter which today represents the attitude not only of the United States but also of Great Britain and of the Soviet Union.
>
> In view of this fact in our considered opinion it would be unfortunate were any of the three governments, now on common ground in the Atlantic Charter, to express any willingness to enter into commitments regarding specific terms of the postwar settlement. Discussions between the several governments looking toward fullest possible agreement on basic policies and toward later arrangements at the proper time and with full public knowledge will of course be expected to continue. Upon the conclusion of hostilities those nations contributing to the defeat of the Hitler forces will join in an effort to restore peace and order. The participation at that time of the Soviet Government will be no less than that of Great Britain and our own. In order not to jeopardize the aims we shall all share in common looking to an enduring peace, it is evident that no commitments as to individual countries should be entered into at this time. It would be unfortunate if we should approach the peace conference thus hampered. Above all there must be no secret accords.

Churchill agreed, writing to Eden in January, 1942, that "there can be no question of settling frontiers until the peace conference."

Throughout the war years Roosevelt and Churchill were held to the principle of postponement by the combined pressures of the Eastern European governments in exile, military advisors motivated by the single-minded purpose of defeating the Axis powers, the requirement of national unity in the successful conduct of the war effort, and Roosevelt's own self-assurance that he could remove the deviations of purpose among the Allies in due time with personal diplomacy. Secretary Hull, moreover, was reluctant to face the great political questions of the war before it was necessary. (*See Document No. 1.*) But what bothered some observant Americans was the danger that Soviet ambition might expand with the success of the Red Army if no agreements were reached while the Russians still required American cooperation. Walter Lippmann analyzed the high cost of procrastination in January, 1945. "A very large part of our present difficulties," he wrote, "may be traced to the policy of reiterating high principles and of postponing the settlement of concrete issues. . . . For the effect of urging postponement in the name of high principles has been to . . . nullify our own influence in favor of moderation and compromise. Thus the more we preached high principles and postponed settlements the greater became the gap between our principles and what was happening."

Divergent Purposes for Germany. Soviet determination to maintain the newly-created hegemony in Eastern Europe flowed as much from the experience of war as from historic ambition. That Russia, unlike the United States and Britain, was invaded by German armies made certain the disruption of Allied interests vis-à-vis Germany with the destruction of Nazi power. Western security interests required nothing of a defeated Germany other than a general settlement which, with minor guarantees against the resurgence of German nationalism, would conform to the principle of self-determination. For the United States and England there was no dichotomy between wartime principles and national purpose. Russian interests, on the contrary, required territorial and political guarantees against the recurrence of direct invasion from the west. In the Soviet occupation and control of Eastern and Central Europe lay the only apparent rewards of victory. To win acceptance of such an altered structure of European politics, the Kremlin had no choice but to extend to the West proposals for the division of Europe into spheres of influence.

The New Balance of Power. What mattered to thoughtful Americans in 1945 was not Soviet ideology, but the new balance of power. In a letter to Hull of May, 1944, Admiral William D. Leahy recognized the changes being wrought in world politics by the Russian victories on the Eastern front. "In appraising possibilities of this nature," he wrote, "the outstanding fact to be noted is the recent phenomenal development of the heretofore latent Russian military and economic strength—a development which seems certain to prove epochal in its bearing on future politico-military international relationships, and which has yet to reach the full scope attainable with Russian resources." Already the forces of the U.S.S.R. had moved from the defensive to the offensive, and were beginning their sweep into Rumania, Hungary, Poland, and the Baltic states. In the months that followed it became clear that Russia, not Britain, would succeed Germany as the major force in European affairs.

In retrospect it was obvious that two world wars had hurried along the fundamental process of bringing the United States and the U.S.S.R. to the forefront of world politics. These wars had dragged a reluctant United States to the center of the world stage as the dominant power of the Western world. During World War I, the Russians, following the devious route of revolution, broke out of those internal restraints imposed by Czarist tradition and began their preparation for industrial and technological expansion. World War I itself eased the way for Russia's new assault on the historic forces that had confined that nation's influence and prestige. The Versailles Conference of 1919 dismembered Turkey and Austria, two of the five empires which had contained Russian expansion in recent times. World War II destroyed what was left of the old balance of power in Eastern and Central Europe. By 1945 Germany was in ruins; England and France were weakened almost beyond recall as major forces in world politics. At last the West, through the process of self-destruction—a process for which Germany must carry the chief responsibility, had removed from Eastern European affairs all five of the great nations which only a long generation earlier appeared capable of limiting Russian ambition with relative ease.

American leadership was scarcely prepared for these vast changes. Since victory was unthinkable without unlimited Soviet effort, a victory in the war was never wholly achievable for the democracies. To pursue a triumph of both strength and principle under such circumstances could only involve Western policy in a tragic irony. Perhaps during the war few Americans detected the contradiction between the encouragement of the Soviets to destroy Nazi power in Eastern Europe and the constant promise made to the American people that the peace settlements would conform to the principles of the Atlantic Charter. Stalin made no secret of his determination to foster governments in Eastern Europe friendly to the U.S.S.R. Never again, he warned Ambassador Averell Harriman, would he tolerate a belt of anti-Soviet governments along Russia's western frontiers. Roosevelt and Churchill simultaneously promised the peoples freed from German domination that they would be permitted self-determination and assured Stalin that the West was cognizant of his interest in pro-Soviet governments along the Russian periphery. Churchill explained Western intentions in February, 1945: "The Poles will have their future in their own hands, with the single limitation that they must honestly follow, in harmony with their allies, a policy friendly to Russia. This is surely reasonable."

Unfortunately, by 1945 the Western powers could no longer guarantee even limited self-determination to the people of Eastern Europe. There was no clear way to defeat the Axis without turning over control of Slavic Europe to Russian armies. By early 1945 Soviet forces, in pushing their way into Germany and Austria, had swept across Poland, Czechoslovakia, Rumania, Bulgaria, and Hungary. In addition, the Soviets had established their influence in Communist-ruled Yugoslavia and Albania. Obviously, there was no power in Europe that could force a Russian withdrawal to her borders of 1939. Nor would there be—short of the rebuilding of the German war machine. Obviously, Russia's new accretion of strength would drive her toward policies designed both to force an acceptance of the new status quo in Eastern and Central Europe and to guarantee her security against a resurgent Germany.

The Yalta Conference. The Yalta Conference of February, 1945, became a traumatic experience because it exposed in one massive revelation, for those who chose to read its lessons, what the United States government had suppressed with remarkable success through three years of war. How could a democratic leadership reiterate the principles of the Atlantic Charter and admit publicly that these principles meant nothing to an ally whose defection would mean failure? It seemed better to dispose of the German problem unencumbered by doubts and permit the Soviet challenge to pass unnoticed under the assumption that it could be disposed of later or perhaps avoided com-

pletely. Even before Roosevelt left for the Crimea late
in January, the State Department made it clear that the
time had passed when the United States could control
events in Eastern Europe. In a sense Western Europe had
given up that control when it failed to protect Czechoslovakia and Poland from German and Soviet encroachment in 1939. Nothing remained with the end of fighting
to counter the Soviet military position except the Russian
signature on the Atlantic Charter. Unless the West chose
to threaten the Soviets with military force, there was little
left in the Western arsenal except paper agreements and
the willingness to resort to moral pressure.

Having lost control of Slavic Europe to Russian armies,
the Western Allies attempted to salvage what they could
of the Atlantic Charter in the form of a Declaration on
Liberated Europe. Under it the Big Three pledged themselves to assist the former Nazi satellites "to solve by
democratic means their pressing political and economic
problems" and to acknowledge "the right of all people to
choose the form of government under which they will
live." This so-called Yalta Charter was Roosevelt's final
and futile effort to prevent the creation of a Soviet sphere
of influence in Eastern Europe.

The Tragedy of a Divided Europe.   Even before the
Yalta Conference, Soviet policy toward Poland had put
the wartime alliance to the test. Early in January, 1945,
a Moscow broadcast announced that the U.S.S.R. was
recognizing the Lublin Committee as the provisional government of Poland. Clearly this group, by Western political standards, was not representative of the Polish people.
Britain and the United States continued to recognize the
exiled Polish government in London. The *Manchester
Guardian* predicted that the Lublin group would win because the Soviets had control of Poland. Roosevelt complained to Stalin on February 6, "It seems to me that it
puts all of us in a bad light throughout the world to have
you recognizing one government while we and the British
are recognizing another in London." At Yalta a few days
later the Soviets promised to include Poles from abroad
in the Lublin government. How this agreement could be
implemented was not evident.

This clear Soviet defiance of the Atlantic Charter in

the first postwar effort at political reconstruction in Eastern Europe produced a wide variety of reactions in the Western world. The London Poles denounced the Yalta communiqué as a violation of the principle of self-determination. Charles Rozmarek, president of the Polish-American Congress, declared: "It is with sorrow, dismay and protest that we greet the decision of the Big Three to give all land east of the so-called Curzon line to Russia in direct contradiction to all sacred pledges of the Atlantic Charter. This tragic revelation is a staggering blow to the cause of freedom." The Chicago *Tribune* observed simply that American morality and diplomacy had hit a new low at Yalta. Meanwhile, the State Department assured the American people that the principles of the Yalta Declaration would be effective in practice; alone they would terminate any danger of spheres of influence in Europe. "The British and Soviet Governments, with the United States," declared James C. Dunn, State Department spokesman, over NBC, "are pledged to consult with each other constantly in every part of liberated Europe." Perhaps Senator Arthur H. Vandenberg's noted speech of January 10, 1945, epitomized the American dilemma. He demanded the right for Americans to criticise Soviet action, but he refused to face the central challenge—that beyond peace the United States would be forced to concede either its principles or its alliance with Russia.

In London Churchill defended the Yalta agreements before the House of Commons late in February as the best that could be obtained. "Only one link in the chain of destiny," he said, "can be handled at a time." On the following day Captain Thorneycroft reminded the House of Commons that the difficulty between East and West was not Poland at all, but rather the growing conflict between American idealism, embodied in the Atlantic Charter, and Russian realism, embodied in the historic advice and ambitions of the Czars. The process of adjusting these differences, he predicted, would be a long and painful one. (*See Document No. 2.*)

Stalin, in lieu of any settlement, proceeded to turn liberated Europe into a Soviet sphere of influence. Late in February he dispatched Soviet diplomat Andrei Vishinski to Bucharest to force King Michael to appoint the

Soviet puppet, Petra Groza, as head of the new Communist-dominated government of Rumania. Early in March, Foreign Minister Vyacheslav Molotov demanded that the old Lublin regime form the core of the provisional government of Poland promised at Yalta. The pattern of Soviet policy was clear. Using his political and ideological identification with local Communist leaders, Stalin gradually established a series of friendly Communist governments in the areas occupied by Soviet troops.

Differences between East and West over Eastern Europe moved quickly beyond the point of reconciliation. Ambassador Harriman reported from Moscow in May, 1945: "I am afraid that Stalin does not and never will fully understand our interest in a free Poland as a matter of principle. The Russian Premier is a realist in all of his actions, and it is hard for him to appreciate our faith in abstract principle. It is difficult for him to understand why we should want to interfere with Soviet policy in a country like Poland which he considers so important to Russia's security unless we have some ulterior motive." What disturbed Churchill was the Soviet policy of creating a distinct zone in Eastern Europe. He wired Truman on May 12, urging some settlement with the Kremlin even at the cost of principle:

> I am profoundly concerned about the European situation. I have always worked for friendship with Russia, but like you, I feel deep anxiety because of their misinterpretation of the Yalta decisions, their attitudes toward Poland, their overwhelming influence in the Balkans . . . and above all their power to maintain very large armies in the field for a long time. . . . Surely it is vital now to come to an understanding with Russia, or see where we are with her, before weakening our armies mortally or retiring to the zones of occupation. . . . Of course we may take the view that Russia will behave impeccably, and no doubt that offers the most convenient solution. To sum up, this issue of a settlement with Russia before our strength has gone seems to me to dwarf all others.

Walter Lippmann voiced the same impatience with the tendency toward drift. He asserted on May 8 that Europe actually was divided into two exclusive spheres of influence, one dominated by the United States and the other

by the U.S.S.R., each limited largely to its own sphere. "No
nation, however strong," he wrote, "has universal world
power which reaches everywhere. The realm in which
each state has the determining influence is limited by
geography and circumstance. Beyond that realm it is
possible to bargain and persuade but not to compel, and
no foreign policy is well conducted which does not recognize these invincible realities."

The American Response. Official Washington had
promised too much and expected too much to recognize
the Soviet sphere of influence. Roosevelt, during his last
weeks as President, saw that the big-power unity for which
he had struggled throughout the war years was eluding him
and the nation. Outwardly he remained optimistic to the
end. Shortly before his death he wired to Churchill: "I
would minimize the general Soviet problem as much as
possible because these problems, in one form or another,
seem to arise every day and most of them straighten
out. . . ." Privately, the President was less sure. In a
series of dispatches to Stalin he reminded the Soviet leader
that in his defiance of wartime agreements he was destroying the unity which the Western world had been led to
expect. "You must believe me when I tell you," he wrote
early in February, "that our people at home look with
a critical eye on what they consider a disagreement between us at this vital state of the war." In an eventual
mood of desperation, Roosevelt wrote to Stalin on April
5, one week before his death: "It would be one of the
greatest tragedies in history if at the very moment of victory now within our grasp such distrust and such lack of
faith should prejudice the entire undertaking after the
colossal losses of life and material and treasure involved."

That vast body of mutual wartime interests, centering in
the quest for victory, which had permitted American
leadership to postpone all fundamental decisions relative
to Soviet intention, no longer existed. But Roosevelt had
simply created no policy for dealing with Stalin's postwar
behavior. During the war Allied decisions had assumed
a cooperative peacetime Russia, principled by Western
standards; in 1945 the Western powers faced a new
Russia, vastly augmented in ambition, aggressiveness, and
size, determined to pursue its separate course in world

affairs. The Soviet challenge was limited, but unmistakable. Any American response that came to grips with the problem had either to recognize the new Soviet hegemony, in an effort to minimize its scope, or to seek the strength to undo it. But Roosevelt's successors, unwilling as he was to abandon principle, yet equally unable to dispose of Soviet power, could only extend into the postwar era the techniques of evasion.

Truman found the answer to the Russian challenge in the determination to stand firm. He informed his cabinet on April 23 that he felt "our agreements with the Soviet Union so far had been a one-way street." He intended, he said, to continue preparations for the San Francisco Conference and "if the Russians did not wish to join us they could go to hell." Vandenberg found enough solace in these words to confide in his diary, "FDR's appeasement of Russia is over." The United States and the U.S.S.R. could live together successfully, the Senator was convinced, "if Russia is made to understand that we can't be pushed around." In May the wartime lend-lease program for Russia was cancelled abruptly. What economic pressure could not achieve seemed well within the capabilities of the atomic bomb. If the bomb worked, the President remarked, "I'll certainly have a hammer on those boys." It was needed, observed the new Secretary of State, James F. Byrnes, not to defeat Japan, but to "make Russia manageable in Europe."

In Europe, however, the administration had no interest in applying the little military force that still remained in its possession. Joseph E. Davies, Truman's special envoy to London, warned him that Churchill was too much concerned with British interests on the Continent. With his advisors concurring, the President decided against using the matter of retirement to agreed zones of occupation for the purpose of bargaining. It seemed to make little difference, for in June the President announced a settlement of the Polish issue, adding confidently that the Russians were anxious to get along peacefully with the American people. Harry Hopkins, on a special mission to Moscow, had convinced Stalin that the United States was not trying to force a government on Poland unfriendly to the U.S.S.R. Ambassador Harriman reached a final agreement on June 22. 1945, to establish a new provisional government for Poland.

The San Francisco Conference. Most Americans found their real hope for a peaceful future in the events at San Francisco, where from April to June, 1945, spokesmen for the victorious nations succeeded in framing the United Nations Charter. For many the U.N. simply became the end of foreign policy. Here at last was the forum before which the law-abiding countries could summon criminal aggressors and demand their compliance with international law.

Yet in the context of big-power rivalry it was clear that the new U.N., like the League of Nations before it, would serve largely as an instrument of evasion. Among sovereign states no international organization can ever be more than an agency of individual national policies. The United Nations could not terminate the struggle for power and prestige among the countries of the world. Nor could it achieve genuine concert in international affairs or force its decisions through collective action on any major power. It could only provide a public forum where nations would add new political instruments to the traditional weapons of diplomacy—where they would resort to legalism in manipulating the procedure of the organization and turn all serious debate into appeals for world sentiment. Since such weapons could have no viable effect on the actual distribution of power in the world, the battles of the U.N. would remain barren. No minority would permit its power or security to be jeopardized by the vote of the majority. Voting could never be as important as the agreement to consult. If the U.N. created an excellent piece of machinery to bring nations together for debate, it did not create a new international order. And nothing would destroy it more quickly than the insistence that it perform as if some new order in international society had actually been established.

The Potsdam Conference. Truman, Churchill, and Stalin met at Potsdam in mid-July, 1945, accompanied by their foreign ministers and military advisors, endowed with the power to establish the foundations of peace. Yalta had been a conference of commanders-in-chief; Potsdam was a meeting of political leaders confronted with the obligation to block out the territorial, economic, and administrative arrangements for reconquered Europe. The conference achieved quick agreement on the establishment of the Council of Foreign Ministers. On the concrete issues of Germany and Eastern Europe there was no possible compromise. Stalin employed every device and agreement to maintain the maximum degree of Soviet prestige, power, and security. When he failed to win concessions, he favored postponement. The Big Three agreed eventually that Germany should be demilitarized, denazified, and democratized. For reparations, each occupying power was authorized to remove property from its own zone and to seize German assets abroad. The four occupying commanders were designated a control council to decide matters affecting Germany as a whole.

Stalin remained totally adamant on the question of Eastern Europe's future. "A freely elected government in any of these East European countries," he admitted simply, "would be anti-Soviet, and that we cannot allow." The United States, Byrnes assured a suspicious Molotov, "sincerely desires Russia to have friendly countries on her borders, but we believe they should seek the friendship of the people rather than of any particular government." His government, said Byrnes, did not wish to become involved in the elections of other countries; it merely desired to join other nations in observing elections in Italy, Greece, Hungary, Rumania, and Bulgaria. Vigorous Western protests against Stalin's unilateral violation of the Yalta agreements resulted in some revision of procedural matters, but left all fundamental issues substantially untouched.

At Potsdam world politics began to assume a bipolar structure. The leading nations, already distrustful of the U.N., were beginning to seek security in their own resources. "As a result," ran John Fischer's judgment in *Harper's* of August, 1945,

> most of the lesser nations are now being drawn by a sort of Law of Political Gravity into the orbit of one or the other of the two Super-Powers. So far neither Russia nor the United States has yet completed its protective belt of satellites. Some areas are being tugged both ways, like small planets caught between two great stars.

As long as the tugging continued, predicted Fischer, the relations between the two great powers would remain tense. The postwar period of "grinding adjustment" had arrived. To avoid war, added Fischer, the United States and the U.S.S.R. had no choice but to accept the sphere of influence of the other. Since Soviet power was dominant in Eastern Europe, eventually the Western nations would be forced to concede with whatever grace they could muster. The unity that remained after Potsdam was limited to rhetoric that could shield the vast conflicts apparent on every issue.

The London Conference. At the Council of Foreign Ministers meeting at London in September, 1945, the trend toward a permanently divided Europe became inescapable. At the conclusion of the conference the London *Observer* warned that there could be no "shirking from the unpleasant fact that, without agreement between Moscow and the West, a line drawn north and south across Europe, perhaps somewhere in the region of Stettin to Trieste, is likely to become more and more of a barrier separating two very different conceptions of life." Soviet intransigence at London had the effect of driving the Western ministers into a solid, opposing bloc. When it became obvious to the Soviets that every issue resulted in the combined opposition of the United States, England, France, and China, they finally broke up the conference by demanding that France and China be excluded from the crucial decisions.

At London Molotov made it clear that Russia's price for cooperation was Western recognition of the new satellite governments of Eastern Europe. Byrnes assured Molotov again that the United States was not interested in seeing anything but governments friendly to the Soviet Union in Eastern Europe. Molotov replied that this could not be true. The Radescu regime in Rumania, which had been hostile to Russia, he said, had received cordial American and British support. Yet, he added, when the Groza government, which was friendly to the Soviet Union, was established, the Western powers had withdrawn their recognition. Byrnes replied that Soviet pressure had forced the Groza regime on the Rumanian people. "Our objective," Byrnes explained, "is a government both friendly to the Soviet Union and representative of all the democratic elements of the country." The Secretary countered Molotov's continuing demand for security against Germany with an offer binding the United States to that nation's demilitarization for twenty-five years. Such a security pact appeared to the Russians less substantial than an arrangement based on their own power. Eventually Byrnes returned to the United States, unable to modify Soviet intransigence on any of the fundamental issues dividing the world.

Byrnes at Moscow.   Without special preparation or Republican advisors, Byrnes traveled to Moscow in December, 1945, against the judgment of veteran diplomats and correspondents. "I believed," he wrote in his defense, "that if we met in Moscow, where I could have a chance to talk to Stalin, we might remove the barriers to the peace treaties. The peace of the world was too important for us to be unwilling to take a chance on securing an agreement after full discussions." Byrnes eventually gained Stalin's acceptance of a peace conference, but he was forced to compromise his London stand.

Byrnes, with his advisors, chiefly Ambassador Harriman and career officer Charles E. Bohlen, was convinced at Moscow that the continued nonrecognition of the Soviet hegemony would achieve nothing for the United States. (In October and November the United States had extended recognition to the provisional governments of Austria and Hungary.) At Moscow, without denying American principles, Byrnes accepted the existing regimes of Rumania and Bulgaria. Stalin agreed to a token representation of pro-Western parties and pledged early free elections. If these agreements represented some retreat from the previous American position, they recognized essentially that the United States had few choices remaining.

The Hardening American Response.   Byrnes' search for a decision at Moscow terminated abruptly the optimistic American attitude toward Russia born of wartime collaboration. Tragically, the continued Soviet determination to maintain political control of Eastern and Central Europe unleashed in the United States a variety of equally determined pressures against any concession of principle.

Truman, in his Navy Day speech of October 27, 1945, declared that this nation would never recognize any government established by force against the freely expressed will of the people. Walter Lippmann retorted that the President's generalizations would do little for negotiations. "We do indeed live in a marvelous age," he added caustically, "having succeeded not only in tapping the sources of atomic energy but the source of moral revelation as well."

Embarrassed by Brynes' concessions at Moscow, Truman dated his break with his Secretary from that conference. He recorded in his *Memoirs:* "My memorandum (January 5, 1946) to Byrnes . . . was the point of departure of our policy. 'I'm tired of babying the Soviets,' I had said to Brynes, and I meant it." Jonathan Daniels, in his biography of Truman, quoted the President as saying, "Byrnes lost his nerve at Moscow." He accused Byrnes of not keeping him informed and of taking to the radio without his permission. Admiral Leahy, Truman's personal Chief of Staff, took the lead in condemning the Moscow Declaration. James V. Forrestal, Secretary of the Navy, lauded the President's firmness and suggested that the United States increase its capabilities to meet new dangers. From Moscow Harriman encouraged the administration to get tougher with the Russians, and in May, 1946, George F. Kennan, Harriman's assistant, was recalled from Moscow to advise the State Department on Russian matters.

But the chief movement for a "get tough" policy centered in Republican leadership. Congressional Republicans had supported Roosevelt's wartime policies and decisions. But by the autumn of 1945 it was quite obvious that the wartime effort had brought the nation far less security and peace than the President had promised or that American expenditures had warranted. Republicans now demanded of Truman what Roosevelt had failed to achieve: a world of justice built on the Atlantic Charter.

Following the collapse of the London Conference, John Foster Dulles, Republican foreign policy spokesman, cautioned a national radio audience that Soviet intransigence was designed to determine if this nation would really hold to its principles. Early in October, 1945, the Senate Foreign Relations Committee pressed Byrnes to "get tough" with the Russians. On November 1 the House of Representatives, with only two Republicans in opposition, passed an appropriations bill barring the use of American funds in the Russian satellites. This bill died in the Senate Appropriations Committee, but it revealed a decided shift in Congress, especially among Republicans, toward the new anti-Soviet attitude. Then on December 5, a committee of House and Senate Republicans issued a policy statement chiding the administration's policy in Eastern Europe:

> We believe in fulfilling to the greatest possible degree our war pledges to small nations that they shall have the right to choose the form of government under which they will live and that sovereign rights and self-government shall be restored to those who have been forcibly deprived of them. We deplore any desertion of these principles.

Following the Moscow Conference, Republican leaders became increasingly critical of the administration's failure to free the countries of Eastern Europe from Soviet influence. Representative Clare Booth Luce, in February, 1946, publicly denounced the Truman leadership for ignoring its commitments to the Atlantic Charter, for the dismemberment of Poland, and for its failure to carry out the principle of self-determination in the Russian satellites. Late that month Vandenberg warned the Senate of the growing rivalry between the United States and the U.S.S.R. He concluded:

> If this is so . . . I assert my own belief that we can live together in reasonable harmony if the United States speaks as plainly upon all occasions as Russia does; if the United States just as vigorously sustains its own purposes and its ideals upon all occasions as Russia does; if we abandon the miserable fiction, often encouraged by our own fellow travelers, that we somehow jeopardize the peace if our candor is as firm as Russia's always is; and if we assume a moral leadership which we have too frequently allowed to lapse. The situation calls for patience and good will; it does not call for vacillation. . . . There is a line beyond which compromise cannot go— even if we once crossed that line under the pressures of the exigencies of war. But how can we expect our alien

friends to know where that is unless we re-establish the
habit of saying only what we mean and meaning every
word we say?

This posture of toughness toward Russia permitted the
Republican leadership to identify itself with the normally
Democratic urban groups of Eastern European and Catholic background. Herein lay the chief significance of the
Soviet issue in American politics. Catholic editors and
writers of Eastern European origin, supported by such
national pressure groups as the Polish-American Congress,
took the lead in charging past American and British policies for the loss of Eastern Europe. Editor James M. Gillis
of the *Catholic World* observed in May, 1946, that "if the
real Poland can never speak again, the shame of the democracies and the futility of the UN are both revealed." The
writer placed the blame on those who led the United States
into war to save Poland from the Nazis and then threw the
country to the Russian wolves. "That's why some of us,
contemptuously branded isolationists," ran his conclusion,
"are chary of assuming international obligations which
we know we cannot fulfill, and which not even the most
rabid interventionists honestly intend to fulfill."

The Problem of Means.   These strident demands for
the triumph of principle held the nation to its inflexible
posture toward the U.S.S.R. But nowhere did they suggest
any course of action which had a serious relationship to
the limitless goals which they created. Few Americans
would have favored decisions more explicit than those pre-
scribed by Vandenberg. When it became obvious that the
new Polish government was involved in a series of political
murders in Poland, Byrnes instructed the American Embassy in Warsaw to "inform the Polish government that
we are relying on that government to take the necessary
steps to assure the freedom and security which are essential to the successful holding of free elections." Vandenberg objected immediately, declaring that it was not
enough to rely on the Polish government to "vindicate
the honor and the pledge of the United States of
America." We must rely, he said, "on our own moral
authority in a world which, in my opinion, craves our
moral leadership." Such firmness did not mean war, he

insisted in a passage reminiscent of the internationalism of
the interwar years:

> It means, first, that we must insistently demand prompt
> and dependable assurances that the Yalta and Potsdam
> pledges in behalf of free elections be effectively fulfilled.
> It means, in other words, that we shall lift the powerful
> voice of America in behalf of the inviolable sanctity of
> international agreements to which we are a party. If this
> does not suffice, it means, then, that we shall scrupulously
> collect our facts; draw our relentless indictment if the
> facts so justify; and present it in the forum of the United
> Nations and demand judgment from the organized con-
> science of the world.

This increasing reliance on moral force permitted national leaders to escape the obvious intellectual dilemma
posed by the simultaneous sustaining of their demands on
Russia and the dismantling of the American military establishment. On matters of national defense the Republicans,
despite their greater expectations of success abroad, were
considerably behind the national administration. The
policy of toughness assured economy-minded isolationists
that they could "gird themselves with the shiny armor of
anti-communism" without encumbering the nation in additional expenditures. Whatever the needs of the hour, demobilization was in the air, and the majority of both
parties accepted the obligation of reducing the size of the
armed forces. Already the dichotomy, familiar enough in
American experience, between the requirements of national performance and the almost total neglect of means,
had become characteristic of the nation's behavior.

Churchill battled this trend in his famous speech at
Fulton, Missouri, in March, 1946. Assuring the nation
that he spoke for himself alone, the British leader alluded
to an *Iron Curtain* descended across the European continent. He did not claim to know the limits of the expansive and proselytizing tendencies of either Russia or
the Communist international. But the challenge, he said,
required a "fraternal association of English-speaking peoples," and "intimate relationships between our military
advisors, leading to a common study of potential dangers,
the similarity of weapons and manuals of instruction, the
interchange of officers and cadets at technical colleges"

and "joint use of all naval and air force bases in the possession of either country all over the world." Russia, he believed, did not desire war, but, he added, "I am convinced that there is nothing they admire so much as strength and there is nothing for which they have less respect than for military weakness." (*See Document No. 3.*)

Truman, although present at Fulton, disclaimed all responsibility for Churchill's speech. White House Press Secretary, Charles G. Ross, reported that the President did not know of its contents, and at the Jackson Day dinner two weeks later the President himself made no reference to it. Thus Truman succeeded in escaping much of the bitter condemnation of Churchill's plea for an Anglo-American alliance. Members of Congress and the American people in general were still reluctant to commit American power permanently to the defense of Europe. Churchill's program appeared to call for a return to power politics and would merely force the Russians to create a countering alliance. To Pearl S. Buck, speaking at Town Hall, Churchill's speech was a catastrophe because it threatened to split the world. The British statesman was hailed and jeered on his procession through New York, and a leftist demonstration outside the dinner hall lasted for two hours. Senator Arthur Capper of Kansas, a noted Republican, took a parting shot at Churchill by charging him with trying to "arouse the people of the United States to commit the country to the task of preserving the far-flung British Empire." What Churchill's speech seemed to indicate was that most Americans, whatever their feeling toward Russia, would retreat from any program that required more of the United States than an appeal to moral disapprobation.

The Paris Conferences of 1946. Byrnes after the Moscow Conference began to respond to the pressures of the right. At a cabinet luncheon late in January he complained that the attacks of Vandenberg and Dulles on his actions were largely partisan. Then in a radio report of February 28, to counter the charges of appeasement, he assumed a position as firm as Vandenberg's (one wit termed this speech the Second Vandenberg Concerto). To reestablish a nonpartisan approach to foreign policy, Byrnes invited both Vandenberg and Tom Connally, the

Democratic leader of the Senate, to accompany him to the Foreign Ministers meeting at Paris late in April. Thereafter, the Republican attacks on Executive leadership began to diminish, whereas at Paris Connally criticised Byrnes for trying too hard to please Vandenberg. Upon his return to the Senate in May, Vandenberg reported that the American delegation had maintained absolute unity on every issue. American policy, he said, was based on the "moralities of the Atlantic and San Francisco charters," as well as "the practical necessities for Europe's rehabilitation." That sort of foreign policy, he concluded, he would support under any administration.

To one high French official, Byrnes at Paris "gave the impression of a clever politician determined not to give an inch." His only concern, it seemed, was to put the onus of deadlock on the Soviet government. Every maneuver exposed another irreconcilable conflict. The Secretary terminated one especially futile session with the observation, "Can we at least agree upon adjourning until Monday?" On another occasion Vandenberg reported that the score for the conference was "no runs, no hits, and a lot of errors (but not by us)." By mid-May Connally observed that both Byrnes and Vandenberg believed United States-Soviet relations had fallen into a bottomless pit. The only alternatives remaining for the West were surrender or recess. In his report to the Senate, Vandenberg insisted that delay was preferable to error. "We can compromise within the boundaries of a principle," he admitted. "We can no longer compromise principles themselves."

When the Paris conference reconvened in July, Byrnes demanded a settlement. He warned Molotov that if there was no agreement on an early meeting of the 21-nation peace conference, the Western nations would proceed to negotiate a separate treaty with Italy. If one world was impossible, the West would simply organize the area outside the Soviet orbit. Byrnes' policy of firmness and patience gradually shifted to one of firmness without patience, for behind American pressure was the determination to reduce the nation's troop strength in Europe. It seems incredible that the Secretary should have been forced to bargain with the Russians at all. As Anne O'Hare

McCormick wrote in July, "When Americans demand in one breath that their government take a firm stand on principle and in the next that the bulk of our forces be withdrawn from Europe, they should not complain of unsatisfactory compromises. We cannot stand and move away at the same time." Despite this apparent impatience, Byrnes won substantial concessions from the Russians on an Italian treaty, with a free city of Trieste and British control of the former Italian colonies.

The Futility of the Moral Response. American "get tough" policy after 1945, which never comprised more than a change of style, satisfied the domestic requirements of a government that had somehow to promise powerful pressure groups and politicians that it would secure the triumph of self-determination. Yet in the new rhetoric lay eventual tragedy, for it convinced too many Americans that there was some special power in words and created the illusion that the choices before the nation in its negotiations with the Soviet Union were much broader than the presence of Red armies in all regions of dispute suggested. The "get tough" attitude gave nothing away, but it assured no settlements on American terms.

Henry A. Wallace, Secretary of Commerce, took the lead in criticizing the nation's stereotyped response to the question of exclusive spheres of influence in Europe. In a memorandum to the President of July 23, he admitted the administration's success in achieving bipartisan cooperation in its new attitudes toward Russia, but he questioned whether unity built on currying conflict abroad was advisable. "I think there is some reason to fear that in our earnest efforts to achieve bipartisan unity in this country," he warned, "we may have given way too much to isolationism masquerading as tough realism in international affairs."

On September 12, at Madison Square Garden, Wallace called for a policy of peaceful competition with Russia. What mattered, he said, were not peace treaties over Greece and the German satellites, but peace between the United States and Russia. "On our part," he said,

> we should recognize that we have no more business in the *political* affairs of Eastern Europe than Russia has in

the *political* affairs of Latin America, Western Europe, and the United States . . . whether we like it or not, the Russians will try to socialize their sphere of influence just as we try to democratize our sphere of influence. This applies also to Germany and Japan. The Russians have no more business in stirring up native Communists to political activity in Western Europe, Latin America, and the United States than we have in interfering with the politics of Eastern Europe and Russia.

Wallace did not regard Russia an immediate danger to Western Europe; for that reason he denied the need of an active policy of force. But he voiced clearly his belief that merely getting tough would not secure the fulfillment of the aspirations of Yalta. Western toughness would always be matched by that of the Kremlin. In the conflict over Eastern Europe, he knew, the Soviets held the overwhelming advantage. Their defense was not based on claims and aspirations, but on physical occupation and military power. Walter Lippmann wondered again why the nation preached high ideals for Eastern Europe when it had established its own sphere of influence in the Pacific north of the equator.

For the Russians Byrnes' continuing reliance on moral force, rather than bargaining, to have his way seemed quite incomprehensible. In *Speaking Frankly,* Byrnes acknowledged that the Russians had analyzed his methods precisely. After one heated session at Paris, Charles E. Bohlen, advisor to the American delegation, remained behind to converse with a member of the Soviet delegation. "The Soviet representative," reported Bohlen, "said it was impossible for him to understand the Americans. They had a reputation for being good traders and yet Secretary Byrnes for two days had been making speeches about principles—talking, he said, like a professor." With all sincerity, the Soviet delegate added, "Why doesn't he stop his talking about principles, and get down to business and start trading?"

Such reliance on moral force created some illusion of ultimate success. Yet as a substitute for concrete policy it comprised largely an escape from responsibility. In December, 1946, Lippmann analyzed succinctly why American action would continue to reap little but futility:

Mr. Byrnes, Mr. Vandenberg, Mr. Connally, and Mr. Truman had been schooled in the Senate, and Mr. Bevin in the Trades Union Congress and in Parliament. Unable to induce or compel M. Molotov by what they regarded as diplomacy, they sought to outvote him, and to arouse public opinion against him. The theory of this procedure was that by bringing issues to a public vote an aroused public opinion would do to the Russians what it has done now and then to Tammany Hall and Mayor Hague, to Mr. Joe Martin and Senator Taft.

But to apply the methods of domestic politics to international politics is like using the rules of checkers in a game of chess. Within a democratic state, conflicts are decided by an actual or a potential count of votes—as the saying goes, by ballots rather than bullets. But in a world of sovereign states conflicts are decided by power, actual or potential, for the ultimate arbiter is not an election but war.

Two disturbing postwar trends, each destroying the illusion of one world, converged during the summer and autumn of 1946. The first was the unbroken increase in tension between East and West. What had begun as a verbal struggle over the future of the Russian satellites had, in the absence of any diplomatic agreements, degenerated into a conflict of immense hostility. Byrnes recognized this alarming quality in the debate raging across Europe. "The thing which disturbs me," he observed late in October, 1946, "is not the lettered provisions of the treaties under discussion but the continued if not increasing tension between us and the Soviet Union." The second trend of 1946 was the further structuring of a bipolar world—an evolution characterized both by the gradual assumption of Western leadership by the United States and the simultaneous conclusion among the lesser countries of the West that the position of neutrality between the giants was no longer tenable. As the astute London *Observer* commented on October 27, 1946: "Our relations with America and Russia are not the same. Those with America, though our views and interests are far from identical, are easy and friendly, and we cannot view America as a potential menace to our existence. The same cannot, unfortunately, be said of Russia. . . ."

For Byrnes the conflict between the United States and

the U.S.S.R. was still sufficiently limited to rule out the rearming of Germany or Japan. Nor had he any desire to break off negotiations with the Soviets. If the postwar experience had been hard on the nerves of diplomats, he wrote, war would be harder on the lives of millions. Diplomacy offered no panaceas. To build a lasting peace required far more diligence and imagination than suggested by the optimism which still anticipated unilateral Russian concessions and the pessimism which anticipated the ultimate triumph of justice only at the end of another war. But the one essential national decision—that of defining American interests in the context of both a divided world and a new balance of power—still awaited a more propitious time.

— 3 —

THE STRUCTURE OF CONTAINMENT

What characterized American foreign policy in the late forties was its gradual retreat from an offensive to a defensive posture. Until 1947 Soviet ambitions appeared limited to regions already under the dominance of the Red Army. The notion that Russia's forward position was only the initial step in a general assault on the free world was scarcely in evidence. It was Western policy, with its avowed purpose of deflating the Soviet hegemony, that maintained a spirit of aggressiveness. Soviet power was finite; its existence was disturbing only to the extent that it underwrote the new Communist regimes of Eastern Europe. The assumption that Stalinist behavior posed a moral rather than a physical challenge created the illusion that a sufficient response lay somewhere in the realm of verbal disapprobation. This permitted American leadership to sustain its expectation of eventual Soviet capitulation at the same time that it continued to reduce the size of the nation's military establishment. Soviet intransigence throughout 1945 and 1946 was more productive of frustration than of fear.

But even the limited conflict of purpose over Eastern Europe, comprising no immediate threat to Western security, eventually forced the West to think in the traditional terms of power politics. To adapt its policies to the new conditions of international life, Western leadership had to evaluate both the strength of the West to protect its interests in a new era of struggle and to define the long-range motivations, intentions, and capabilities of the U.S.S.R. The isolationist tendencies in American attitudes toward world affairs—the inclination to drift under the assumption that the nation was really quite invincible and that most problems eventually resolved themselves without American involvement—predicted a slow and painful adjustment in both the material and conceptual framework of national policy. That the Kremlin presented a challenge to American complacency was clear, but beyond acknowledging a divided world Washington officials seemed incapable of agreeing on either the character or the magnitude of the Russian threat.

The Question of Soviet Intentions.   President Harry S. Truman and his advisors attempted to parry Soviet demands abroad and reassure the American people at home. The first eighteen months of postwar maneuvering produced a series of Allies treaties with such former Nazi satellites as Italy, Hungary, Bulgaria, and Rumania, but these agreements scarcely infringed on Soviet dominance behind the Iron Curtain. In his address before the U.N. General Assembly in October, 1946, the President minimized the apparent East-West conflict. "The war has left many parts of the world in turmoil," he admitted. "Differences have arisen among the Allies. It will not help us to pretend that this is not the case. But it is not necessary to exaggerate the differences. . . . Above all, we must not permit differences in economic and social systems to stand in the way of peace either now or in the future." But in his State of the Union message three months later, Truman issued a warning to the Congress. "We live in a world in which strength on the part of the peace-loving nations is still the greatest deterrent to aggression . . . ," he said. "When a system of collective security under the United Nations has been established we shall be willing to lead in collective disarmament, but, until such a system becomes a reality, we must not again allow our weakness to invite attack." Clearly, Soviet behavior had prompted the administration to examine the whole question of Western security vis-à-vis the U.S.S.R. Behind this obvious shift toward a stronger policy at the beginning of 1947 was the crystallization of the administration's concept of Soviet intentions.

Russian experts in the West had begun their search of the Soviet past for clues which might expose that nation's long-range objectives. George F. Kennan wrote from Moscow in February, 1946: "The Kremlin's neurotic view of world affairs is the traditional and instinctive Russian sense of insecurity. . . . Russian rulers . . . have learned to seek security only in patient but deadly struggle for the total destruction of rival power, never in compacts and compromises with it." Kennan warned the administration that the Kremlin would exert unrelenting pressure on the international system in an effort to undermine its opposition. It would accept no permanent *modus vivendi* with the United States until it had achieved the disruption of Western society. "This political force," ran Kennan's conclusion, "has complete power of disposition over the energies of one of the world's greatest peoples and the resources of the world's richest national territory." No longer, he believed, could the West escape a long-term struggle for power and prestige with the Soviet Union, but he carefully avoided any suggestion of policy that would terminate the struggle on Western terms.

Western Weakness. Soviet intransigence soon convinced Western leaders that not even Western Europe was immune to either Communist infiltration or direct Soviet attack. The precipitate demobilization of British and American troops had created a military vacuum on the continent. By 1947 the United States Congress had reduced the peacetime strength of the nation's armed forces to 1,550,000 men and had instructed the Pentagon to contract even this number to slightly over a million before the end of the year. The U.S.S.R. still had six million under arms in 1946 and had already retooled its aircraft industry.

Only the monopoly in atomic weapons gave the United States any military capability comparable to that of Russia.

Even more obvious than the decline of Western military power was the dislocation of the Western European economies. The vast reduction of European productivity, plus the shortage of capital to rebuild it, created such an enormous dollar gap in trade with the United States that the European continent by 1947 was on the verge of bankruptcy. Inflation merely widened the dollar gap. Britain no longer had the financial resources to pay for the heavy importation of vital food and raw materials. In February, 1947, the British government issued a White Paper on economic conditions which the London *Times* described as "the most disturbing statement ever made by the British government." Drought destroyed much of France's wheat crop in 1946; a severe winter left little wheat for the 1947 harvest. Elsewhere Western Europe had come within a hairsbreadth of total economic collapse. Europe was, Churchill recalled later, "a rubble heap, a charnel house, a breeding ground of pestilence and hate." Everywhere agricultural production was low, factories were closed, and millions drifted about, unemployed. *The New York Times* reported in February, 1947, that severe food shortages confronted victor and vanquished nations alike. Thriving on such chaos, the Communist parties of Western Europe were in the political ascendancy. For Western Europe the first line of defense against the dual forces of starvation and communism was the undiminished productivity of the United States.

The Truman Doctrine. Several factors converged early in 1947 to place American policy vis-à-vis the U.S.S.R. on the defensive. First came the conviction that the Kremlin, if concerned in its diplomacy with the stability of a divided Europe, actually represented a long-term danger to the entire structure of Western civilization. The recognition of Europe's economic and military collapse merely confirmed the trend toward a new mood of fear. The immediate Soviet challenge was no longer the simple defiance of wartime principles in Eastern and Central Europe; it was now the threat of further Russian expansion into the confusion that lay beyond that nation's new imperial frontiers.

Greece and Turkey, both strategically important to the defense of Western Europe, were the principal points of danger. Greece was in a state of complete economic exhaustion. Greek Communists, moreover, had mounted a guerrilla attack on the British-sponsored conservative government. So fragile was the Athens regime that its very existence depended on occupying British forces. Then in February, 1947, the British Embassy in Washington informed the Truman administration that Britain could no longer afford to carry the economic and military burden of keeping Greece out of Communist hands. General George C. Marshall, Secretary of State since January, 1947, recognized the significance of the British withdrawal. Unless the United States assumed the former British commitments, he warned, the pro-Soviet elements in Greece would take over the country.

Truman agreed with Marshall on the requirement of economic relief for Greece and Turkey. Marshall, with the approval of the President, assigned the task of formulating a new American policy to Under Secretary of State Dean G. Acheson. Late in February, to assure Congressional support, the President held a briefing session during which Marshall and Acheson explained to Congressional leaders the possible consequences of a Communist takeover in Greece. Vandenberg advised the President that if he wanted an aid program for Greece and Turkey he had no choice but to appear before Congress in person and "scare hell out of the country."

To many Washington officials the struggle for Greece was the opening round of a vast ideological struggle between Soviet communism and Western democracy. So Vandenberg regarded it. Forrestal asserted at a cabinet meeting early in March that if the United States would win the competition, it would "have to recognize it as a fundamental struggle between our kind of society and the Russians' and that the Russians would not respond to anything but power."

Truman's message to Congress, on March 12, 1947, defined the conflict between the United States and the U.S.S.R. in broad ideological terms and announced this nation's intention to go to the assistance of free governments everywhere. (*See Document No. 4.*) "At the present moment in world history," he declared, "nearly every nation must choose between alternative ways of life. The choice is not often a free one. . . . I believe that it must be the policy of the United States to support free peoples who are resisting attempted subjugation by armed minorities or by outside pressures." He called for a Congressional appropriation of $400 million for economic and military aid to Greece and Turkey. Beyond these two countries the so-called Truman Doctrine was simply a vague and indeterminate commitment to support freedom.

In general the Truman speech had the desired effect upon the nation; it received praise from much of Congress and the press. But some thoughtful Americans criticised the new doctrine for confusing the issue between the United States and the Soviet Union and for reducing the American commitment at a time of trial to vague generalities. Western security demanded the prevention of further Russian expansion. But the President's message identified American interest in Greece and Turkey, not with the maintenance of the European balance of power, but with the defense of freedom even where it scarcely existed. The Truman Doctrine seemed to promise salvation to the world. It perpetuated the nation's habit of refusing to separate what was essential from what was desired. Kennan objected to the President's reference to an ideological struggle between two ways of life and to the open-end commitment to aid free peoples everywhere. To Walter Lippmann the new policy was so general that it had no visible limits. He reminded the national leadership that crusade was not a policy. "A policy, as distinguished from a crusade," he wrote, "may be said to have definite aims, which can be stated concretely, and achieved if the estimate of the situation is correct. A crusade, on the other hand, is an adventure which even if its intentions are good, has no limits because there is no concrete program. To substitute specific aims for vague hostilities is the statesman's business in a time of trouble and danger."

Congress straddled the issue of the Truman Doctrine's meaning. James Reston of *The New York Times* wrote on March 23 that Congress was "neither repudiating the broad principle laid down in the Truman Doctrine . . .

nor following the implications of that principle to the end." Vandenberg, chairman of the Senate Foreign Relations Committee following the 1946 Republican sweep, steered the President's aid measure through Congress without difficulty. By May it had passed both houses of Congress and had become the official policy of the United States. To the extent that the Truman Doctrine comprised a feasible effort to keep Greece and Turkey in the Western bloc, it coincided with American security interests in Europe. To the extent that it promised the eventual triumph over communism, it comprised a moral crusade that would both falter before its impossible goals and prevent any negotiated settlement with the Kremlin. Under the conviction that the source of conflict between the two great powers was not Russian imperialism but international communism, the East-West struggle finally transcended Eastern Europe to blanket the entire globe.

The Marshall Plan. Whatever the ultimate necessity of facing Moscow's ideological challenge, the immediate issue of 1947 was the concrete one of stopping further Soviet expansion in Europe. From this objective evolved the American policy of containment, defined with some precision by Kennan in his article, "The Sources of Soviet Conduct," written under the pseudonym of "Mr. X" in the July, 1947, issue of *Foreign Affairs*. Kennan offered three postulates regarding Soviet beliefs and expectations. The first of these was the Kremlin's acceptance of a fundamental antagonism between capitalism and communism which ruled out any community of interests between the U.S.S.R. and the nations of the West. Second, the Soviets believed that since capitalism in this competition was doomed, there was no need of engaging in all-out war. Third, the Soviet assumption of Kremlin infallibility rendered useless any effort to argue with Russian diplomats, for all important decisions were made at the top level.

But Kennan anticipated a time of successful United States-Soviet diplomacy. The Russian economy, he believed, was basically weak and would force the Kremlin to concede eventually to Western economic superiority. Kennan declared that there was a strong possibility "that Soviet power, like the capitalist world of its conception, bears within it the seeds of its own decay, and that the sprouting of these seeds is well advanced." This led the Russian expert to propose a quiet and restrained policy of containment. He summarized his position with some cogency:

> In these circumstances it is clear that the main element of any United States policy toward the Soviet Union must be that of a long-term, patient but firm and vigilant containment of Russian expansive tendencies. It is important to note, however, that such a policy has nothing to do with outward histrionics: with threats or blustering or superfluous gestures of outward "toughness."

Kennan's effort to extricate American foreign policy from its ideological context was reflected in the proposals of the new Policy Planning Staff, established in the State Department in April, 1947, under his leadership, on the matter of the Marshall Plan. In the spring of 1947 William L. Clayton, Marshall's chief advisor on economic affairs, reported after a six weeks' survey that the United States had persistently underestimated the wartime damage to Europe's economy. Only an expanded program of American aid could save Western Europe from economic and political disaster. The Policy Planning Staff favored such a program but encouraged the Secretary to direct any national effort toward the concrete problems of poverty and hunger, not toward the eradication of communism.

Under Secretary Acheson, in a speech before the Delta Council at Cleveland, Mississippi, on May 8, 1947, warned the nation that it must undertake the economic reconstruction of Europe. Acheson, substituting for the President, was clearly announcing the burgeoning program of the administration. His speech, unlike the Truman Doctrine, did not declare ideological war on communism, but Acheson defined the American intention. "Free people," he said, "who are seeking to preserve their independence and democratic institutions and human freedoms against totalitarian pressures, either internal or external, will receive top priority for American reconstuction aid."

Late in May, Marshall received the policy recommendations for an economic aid program for all Europe from the Policy Planning Staff. These recommendations became the basis of his momentous speech at Harvard University on June 5. The Secretary again spoke of the needs of the European countries. "It is logical," he said, "that the United States should do whatever it is able to do to assist in the return of normal economic health in the world, without which there can be no political stability and no assured peace." Leaving behind all ideological implications, Marshall followed the outline developed by the Policy Planning Staff. "Our policy," he declared, "is directed not against country or doctrine, but against hunger, poverty, desperation, and chaos." Marshall offered American aid to all nations which would cooperate in the program. The Marshall Plan, as the Secretary's proposals came to be called, demanded that the initiative be taken by the European nations as they determined their own needs. (*See Document No. 5.*)

Britain and France responded to Marshall's proposal enthusiastically. Late in June Molotov met with the British and French foreign ministers to discuss the possibilities for an over-all European economic recovery program. That the Russians appeared serious was demonstrated by the eighty economic advisors who accompanied Molotov to Paris. But during the talks, Molotov received a communication from Moscow that terminated all Russian involvement in the program. Thereafter, the Soviet leaders condemned the Marshall Plan as American capitalistic imperialism. Undaunted, Britain and France, early in July, sent invitations to 22 European countries to meet in Paris to discuss Europe's economic requirements. Eight Iron Curtain countries, under heavy Soviet pressure, refused to attend. Eventually the Western nations agreed on their specific needs; the United States Congress responded in 1948 with the first of a series of extensive appropriations. So successful was the new program that by mid-century Western Europe was not only on the road to recovery but had already, in many categories, reached or exceeded prewar production figures. The Marshall Plan, carefully designed to blur the division of Europe, resulted, because of Soviet intransigence, in a program that appeared to have but one purpose—to build centers of strength in a general policy of containment.

Continued Soviet Pressure in Europe.   Two events

of 1948 deepened the East-West conflict by demonstrating the willingness of the U.S.S.R. to employ its power and geographical advantages to undermine what remained of the Western position along its periphery. The first of these episodes was the Communist coup d'état in Czechoslovakia in February. After the war Czechoslovakia held an anomalous position in European affairs. It was, like Berlin, an area of free government behind the Iron Curtain. Soviet influence in Czech affairs was obvious as early as 1947 when that nation refused to cooperate with the Marshall program. For many in the State Department the fall of the Czech government in 1948 was expected, especially since the Communist Party commanded a large plurality in the national Parliament. President Edward Benes was leader of the National Socialists, the largest of the non-Communist parties, but the Premier and other members of the cabinet were Communists, including the Minister of the Interior who controlled the police. Non-Communist leaders threatened to break up the coalition which permitted the Communists to control the cabinet if Communists were permitted to dominate the police establishment. When the Premier refused to comply with these demands, the non-Communist members of the cabinet resigned. The Communist Party, controlling the police, forced the Social Democrats to join them in forming a new government. When Benes recognized the new cabinet, the coup was all but completed.

Informed Americans reacted violently to the fall of Czechoslovakia, not only because that nation had served as a bridge between East and West but also because they recalled how Hitler, using similar pressures, had seized that nation ten years earlier to inaugurate a general assault against his enemies. The Chicago *Tribune* observed late in February, "The American people can very well reflect that this is where they came in. It was ten years ago this fall that the independence of Czechoslovakia was sacrificed at Munich." Former Ambassador to Russia Harriman warned, "There are aggressive forces in the world coming from the Soviet Union which are just as destructive in their effect on the world and our own way of life as Hitler was, and I think are a greater menace than Hitler was."

If this could happen to Czechoslovakia, why not elsewhere? "There is no reason to expect," declared *The New York Times* on February 26, "that Czechoslovakia will be the last target of Russo-Communist expansion." Truman reminded the nation that the Soviet Union and its agents had "destroyed the independence and democratic character of a whole series of nations in eastern and central Europe." Now it was clear that they intended to extend their ruthless course of action "to the remaining free nations of Europe. . . ." The fall of Czechoslovakia to Communist leadership seemed to prove the addage that no nation could do business with the Kremlin without signing its own death warrant. It not only made the U.S.S.R. appear strangely insidious but also created the illusion that the unknown force—communism—had the power to topple governments and convey nations into the Soviet camp. It aggravated the fears and enforced the convictions of those who viewed the East-West struggle in purely ideological terms.

The Soviet blockade of West Berlin in June, 1948, severing all land and water communications between that city and the Western zones of Germany, demonstrated the Soviet inclination to employ force to counter the shifts in Western attitudes and policies toward the defeated power of World War II. For the Kremlin, intent on keeping Germany a cipher in European politics, the only acceptable Allied policy toward that nation was one that would preserve the four distinct zones of occupation and limit the growth of the German economy. But increasingly after 1945 the Western occupying powers determined to reconstruct the Germany under their control both economically and politically. In his speech at Stuttgart in September, 1946, Secretary Byrnes had suggested a change in American policy. "The time has come," he declared, "when the zonal boundaries should be regarded as defining only the areas to be occupied for security purposes by the armed forces of the occupying powers and not as self-contained economic and political units." He implied that if the Soviets refused to cooperate in a new policy toward Germany, aimed at the political and economic unity of that country, the Western powers would merge their own zones. He even suggested the establishment of a provisional German government. In December, 1946, the British and American governments joined their zones economically and assigned increasing numbers of Germans to important administrative posts. In this new era of East-West conflict the wartime policy of unconditional surrender appeared remote and ill-advised.

At the Council of Foreign Ministers meeting at Moscow in March, 1947, the Soviets attempted to prevent the merger of the Western zones into one political entity outside their control by offering a unified Germany on the basis of partial Soviet control of the Ruhr. When Marshall countered with the proposition that the Big Four maintain joint control over both the Ruhr and Upper Silesia, Molotov withdrew his proposal, preferring thereafter to rebuke the West for attempting to rebuild a West German republic as an ally against Russia. At Moscow the Soviets clarified their conditions for German unification. It would come only when the Western powers had withdrawn their occupation forces from that nation.

Unable to control the trend toward the rebuilding of an independent and powerful West Germany, the Kremlin in the spring of 1948 began to restrict the traffic between Berlin, the West German outpost one hundred miles behind the Iron Curtain, and West Germany itself. General Lucius D. Clay, the American commander in Germany, warned the administration in Washington that any retreat from Berlin would expose the West to Soviet blackmail until communism would run rampant. "I believe that the future of democracy," he said, "requires us to stay." Continued Soviet restriction culminated in June with the establishment of a complete blockade. Rather than concede their right of access to the city, the Allies resorted to a massive air lift to supply the beleaguered population. This permitted the West to maintain its position in West Berlin without resorting to armed force. During the negotiations which followed, Stalin assured the Western Allies that Russia respected the Western right of access. It was clear, however, that the Kremlin hoped to prevent the establishment of a West German government by making this the price for lifting the blockade. But the West responded by expanding the air lift until it became evident to the Soviets that the blockade gave them little bargaining power. By February, 1948, Stalin withdrew his opposition to the establishment of a West German government. During May, after several weeks of secret negotiations, the blockade was lifted.

The North Atlantic Treaty Organization. These demonstrations of Soviet aggressiveness magnified Western European fears of Soviet power. For many European leaders the question no longer was one of pushing the Soviets out of the satellites; it was now a matter of preventing Soviet encroachment on free Europe. During March, 1948, in their quest for greater military security against the Soviet danger, Great Britain, France, the Netherlands, Belgium, and Luxembourg signed the Brussels Pact of mutual defense. Thereupon these nations approached the United States for the required military support. President Truman, thoroughly committed to the defense of Western Europe, framed an immediate appeal to Congress: "This development deserves our full support. I am confident that the United States will, by appropriate means, extend to the free nations the support which the situation requires." Congress endorsed the President's views by passing the Vandenberg Resolution of June, 1948, by a vote of 64 to 4, thus preparing the nation for a formal military alliance with the countries of the Atlantic world.

Less than ten months later, in April, 1949, the five members of the Brussels Pact, with the United States, Canada, Denmark, Iceland, Italy, Portugal, and Norway signed the North Atlantic Treaty with ceremonies in Washington. Article 5 set forth the primary obligations of the signatories:

> The Parties agree that an armed attack against one or more of them in Europe or North America shall be considered an attack against them all; and consequently they agree that, if such an armed attack occurs, each of them, in exercise of the right of individual or collective self-defense recognized by Article 51 of the Charter of the United Nations, will assist the Party or Parties so attacked by taking forthwith, individually and in concert with the other Parties, such action as it deems necessary, including the use of armed force, to restore and maintain the security of the North Atlantic area.

Strategically, NATO was dependent on the sword and the shield—a combination of massive air retaliatory power and active troops designed to withstand any initial aggression against Western Europe. To secure the necessary air and naval bases for deterring Soviet aggression, the United States, in cooperation with its allies, prepared to reactivate the American bases in Britain, rebuild the wartime bases in North Africa and West Germany, and establish new bases within the territorial jurisdiction of other NATO members.

Dean G. Acheson, who succeeded Marshall as Secretary of State in January, 1949, seized the burgeoning policies of the administration and proceeded to mold them into one immovable defense against the U.S.S.R. What mattered to him was essentially the power and unity of the Atlantic community. If the Kremlin, he repeated, ever succeeded in breaking up the Western coalition, it would have a free hand in dealing with all the nations of the world. In April the new Secretary appeared before the Senate Foreign Relations Committee to defend the newly-formed North Atlantic Pact. NATO, he said, was a defensive alliance—an agency designed primarily to carry out the purpose of the United Nations Charter. But he refused to dodge the issue of involvement. "If you ratify the Pact," he told the Senators, "it cannot be said that there is no obligation to help, but the extent, the manner, and the timing is up to the honest judgment of the parties." After considerable debate, the Senate ratified the treaty in July.

Next Acheson argued vigorously for the expansion of the NATO military establishment. "The first line of defense is still in Europe," he told the nation in August, 1949, "but our European allies today do not have the military capacity to hold the line. The shield behind which we marshaled our forces to strike decisive blows for the common cause no longer exists. In that sense, the United States is open to attack on its own territory to a greater extent than ever before." Since Europe's vulnerability increased the danger of war, military assistance to the NATO countries would strengthen international peace as well as American security. Behind the new armament program was the essential purpose of placing more power in the hands of those nations concerned with stability than the Soviets could assemble in support of their aggressive ventures. (*See Document No. 6.*)

Few Americans doubted the wisdom of a strong military posture toward the U.S.S.R. in 1950, for there was no apparent alternative. To Western Europeans, American policies alone sustained the Atlantic Alliance. First, the leadership of the United States in atomic weapons was a genuine source of security against the enormous Russian military capacity on the ground. Second, the economic weakness of Western European nations made United States economic aid a serious necessity. Third, the intransigence of Stalinist policies made Russia appear a dangerous and constant threat to the independence of Western Europe. Either the nations of the West would accept the support of the United States or they would face national suicide. NATO was built on the solid foundation of common interest in building defenses against a known antagonist.

Yet any anticipation that the Western alliance would force a rapid change in Soviet purpose had evaporated before the organization was fully ratified. During 1949 the Soviets broke the United States' atomic monopoly. Thereafter the task of bringing overwhelming power to bear on the Soviet Union to force concessions short of war became totally impossible. At best Western military policy might limit Soviet expansion and gain time during which any internal dilemmas within the Soviet system might either produce a total collapse or at least force some accommodation with Western purpose.

The New Far Eastern Balance of Power. At midcentury, when the nation had adjusted in some measure to the Russian challenge in Europe, it discovered suddenly that postwar events in the Far East had terminated the perennial American effort to create a stable Orient around the China of Chiang Kai-shek. During the war the United States had saved Chiang from the Japanese; after 1945 it seemed incapable of saving him from his internal enemies, the Chinese Communists under Mao Tse-tung. Faced with a bitter civil war in China, Ambassador Patrick J. Hurley resigned in November, 1945, charging that the Foreign Service career officers were sympathetic with the Chinese

Reds and that the administration had failed to make public its purpose for China. Byrnes replied to Hurley's charges on December 7. "During the war," he recalled, "the immediate goal of the United States in China was to promote a military union of the several political factions in order to bring their combined power to bear upon our common enemy, Japan. Our long-range goal, then as now . . . is the development of a strong, united, and democratic China."

To bring the desired peace and unity to China, Truman dispatched General George C. Marshall to China in December, 1945, to seek a coalition government. Thereafter the administration turned over the direction of American Far Eastern policy to this soldier-statesman. Throughout 1946 Marshall pursued the illusive objective of achieving some reconciliation between the Chinese Nationalists and the Chinese Communists. Until the time of his return to the United States early in 1947, when he succeeded Byrnes as Secretary of State, Marshall had found both groups in China hopelessly intransigent. Democracy in China, he concluded, required the triumph of that nation's liberal elements.

Marshall's failure to secure American interests in China exposed the administration to partisan attack, for China policy had been the creation of the Executive, not Congress. By 1947 Republican leaders, cognizant of Chiang's declining fortunes, termed American China policy bankrupt and demanded stronger action. Republican pressure led to the mission of General Albert C. Wedemeyer to China in the summer of 1947. His report, which both recommended additional aid to the Kuomintang and admitted that the Nationalist government had little chance of success, was so confusing that Marshall repressed it. Some critics demanded the extension of the Truman Doctrine to China, but Marshall refused to budge from his purpose of limited involvement in the Chinese civil war. China, he reminded the nation, was 45 times as large with 85 times as many people as Greece. To maintain Chiang in power, he predicted, would require billions of dollars and millions of American lives. Democrats in Congress sat mutely, hoping that Marshall's prestige would carry their party through the threatening political battle over the alleged loss of China. Finally, the administration in 1948 accepted a heavy Congressional appropriation for aid to Chiang under the Marshall Plan and, terminating its effort to achieve a coalition government, tied American policy firmly to the Kuomintang. Still Marshall rejected both Republican demands for intervention and Madam Chiang Kai-shek's eleventh-hour plea for help in December, 1948.

When Chiang's collapse appeared imminent in February, 1949, the President called Acheson, Vandenberg, and Vice President Alben Barkley to the White House to formulate a policy that would forestall Congressional criticism. Vandenberg opposed desertion of the Nationalists for fear that the United States would "never be able to shake the charge that we [were] the ones who gave poor China the final push into disaster." Unable to formulate a long-range policy for China, the administration continued to ship moderate quantities of aid to the nationalists but in every other respect maintained a free hand.

Chiang's final defeat during the late months of 1949 loomed so large on the immediate diplomatic and political horizon that the administration felt compelled to explain it to the American people. In August it published the famous China White Paper, a bulky document which attempted to prove that the upheaval in China was the result of massive internal changes over which the United States had no control. Acheson summarized the administration's defense of its policies in one terse statement: "Nothing that this country did or could have done within the reasonable limits of its capabilities would have changed the result, nothing that was left undone by this country has contributed to it." Before the National Press Club in January, 1950, the Secretary again summarized his concept of the upheaval within China: "The Communists did not create this condition. They did not create this revolutionary spirit. They did not create a great force which moved out from under Chiang Kai-shek. But they were shrewd and cunning to mount it, and to ride this thing into victory and into power." (*See Document No. 7.*) Many Americans who knew something of events in China found Acheson's analysis reassuring. The object of American policy in the Orient, declared the Washington *Post* on January 10, "should be to drive a wedge between authentic nationalism and aggressive communism. This is a job that is essentially diplomatic, requiring the pooling of American wisdom and effort, for Asia is going to be the problem of the century."

In Congress, however, the Nationalist China bloc mobilized to force its program on the nation. On January 2, 1950, Senator William F. Knowland of California released a letter from Herbert Hoover which declared that the United States should support the Kuomintang on Formosa and develop a policy to return China to the road of freedom. Truman countered three days later with the statement that the United States had no intention of becoming involved further in China's civil war by establishing bases on Formosa or by utilizing American armed forces to protect the Nationalist government. Chiang would receive economic but not military aid. Acheson warned the nation that the persistent effort to tie American policy to Chiang would isolate the United States diplomatically and "mobilize the whole of Asia's millions solidly against [it]."

Senator Joseph McCarthy of Wisconsin quickly submerged the China question even more deeply in the mire of partisan politics. In February, 1950, without presenting any evidence, he captured the headlines with the charge that the State Department was "thoroughly infested" with Communists. The Senator's sensational accusations at Wheeling, West Virginia, supplied the rationale which tied the unlimited expectations of a counter-revolution in China to the concept of limited American expenditures. By placing the responsibility for Chiang's failure on American leadership, he discovered the argument which would permit a show of aggressiveness in Asia without the corresponding assumption of any expensive military commitment. If the United States had failed to control the Chinese revolution, it meant simply that the State Department was full of Communists. With their removal from office the nation could anticipate the return of the Nationalists to power over all China. Supported by this rationale as well as by much of the Republican Party, the supporters of Chiang Kai-shek in the United States suddenly found themselves in an unshakable position to determine American China policy. Such relentless pressures within the nation permitted the Truman administration no more freedom to recognize the new balance of power in the Orient than it had been permitted, in its European policies, to recognize the new balance of power in Europe.

War in Korea. North Korean aggression across the 38th parallel in June, 1950, brought the entire problem of containment into focus. To the administration this aggression was nothing less than the beginning of a general Communist assault on the free world. "The attack upon the Republic of Korea," the President warned the nation, "makes it plain beyond all doubt that the international Communist movement is prepared to use armed invasion to conquer independent nations." Everywhere Washington officials accused the Kremlin of initiating the attack. If aggression succeeded in Korea, it would be repeated elsewhere until it rendered a third world war inescapable. To prevent attacks in Southeast Asia, the President increased American military assistance to the Philippines and Indochina, and ordered the Seventh Fleet to defend Formosa.

This fear engendered by the Korean War permitted the administration to extract from Congress defense measures which it had urged repeatedly throughout the previous year. In June, 1950, Acheson had appeared before Congress to request one billion dollars to strengthen the defenses of Western Europe. In August the administration added almost four billion to its requirements. Congress, having stalled at the first request, approved the second with one opposing vote in the House and none in the Senate.

Simultaneously, the Truman administration brought its program for rearming West Germany, established as the Federal German Republic in June, 1949, to a successful conclusion. In May, 1950, John J. McCloy, retiring High Commissioner for Germany, declared bluntly that German troops were required for the defense of Europe. In September the Foreign Ministers of the United States, the United Kingdom, and France, responding to the shock of the Korean War, agreed that the re-creation of a German national army would serve the best interests of both Germany and Western Europe. They authorized the new German government at Bonn to establish its own foreign office and enter into diplomatic relations with foreign countries.

China's entry into the Korean War in November, 1950, tended to prove the administration's assumption that the Communist threat of aggression was world-wide. If the new assault was successful in Korea, ran a White House press release in December, "we can expect it to spread through Asia and Europe to this hemisphere. We are fighting in Korea for our own national security and survival." Because the danger was world-wide, it was all the more essential that Congress increase the combined military strength of the free nations. In December, the NATO Council unanimously asked the President of the United States to select a Supreme Commander. Truman responded by naming General Dwight D. Eisenhower, then president of Columbia University, to the task of translating military plans into armed forces in being. Despite its importance in official thought, the Korean War did not alter the Europe-first orientation of the Truman administration. It saw the chief deterrent to Communist expansion in the collective forces of the North Atlantic community, not in any all-out involvement of American power in the struggle against Communist forces in the Far East.

During its initial phases the Korean War had been popular in the United States and claimed vigorous bipartisan support. But when the mainland Chinese propelled the war into a long, dreary, military stalemate, critics of the Truman administration found the arguments which rendered the war the unnecessary consequence of past decisions. The United States, they charged, had invited the aggression in Korea both by failing to create an army in South Korea capable to matching the power of the Communist-led forces of North Korea and by excluding both Korea and Formosa from the perimeter which the United States would defend against military attack. The North Koreans, declared Senator Robert A. Taft of Ohio, merely took the administration at its word. "They knew that we had permitted the taking over of China by the Communists," he added, "and saw no reason why we should seriously object to the taking over of Korea. The Korean War and the problems which arise from it are the final result of the continuous sympathy toward communism which inspired American policy."

Under the pressure of events in Asia and partisan attacks on past decisions in China, the American attitude toward Peiping began to harden into one of extreme antagonism. In February, 1951, the United States managed to push a resolution through the U.N., by a vote of 44 to 7 with 9 abstentions, which branded the mainland Chinese aggressors in Korea. The intensity of the Republican attack on the Korean War increased markedly in April, 1951, when President Truman recalled General Douglas MacArthur from his Pacific command for criticising publicly the limited war policies of the administration. During the Congressional hearings which followed the General's return to the United States, the Senators extracted from Secretary Acheson the promise that he would not recognize the Peiping regime or permit the United Nations to do so. This promise followed, ironically, the Secretary's long and brilliant defense of American policy in China which no one challenged. Acheson never intended that the policy of nonrecognition should continue indefinitely beyond the termination of the war.

For the Truman administration the Korean War gradually became a political liability of incalculable proportions. Yet there was no escape from its burdens. Any armistice required some recognition of the military stalemate which would leave Korea divided and the Chinese successful in preventing United States armed forces from reaching the Chinese frontier. Politically the President was too weak at home to negotiate such a peace. But any struggle for victory would mean enormous casualties and the danger of a general war in the Far East. To most Americans this decision was equally unacceptable. Only the election of Dwight D. Eisenhower to the presidency extracted the nation from its dilemma, for in July, 1953, he was permitted to accept an armistice on terms which Truman could not have accepted without being termed an appeaser.

Not until the Korean War demonstrated the strength and aggressiveness of mainland China, did American leadership accept the necessity of building an alliance system in Asia. In August and September, 1951, the Truman administration negotiated mutual defense treaties with the Philippines, Australia, and New Zealand. Also in September, 1951, it signed a similar pact with Japan which, although it placed no obligation on the United States, conveyed to this nation the right to maintain land, air, and naval forces in and about Japan.

Means Without Ends. Despite the considerable success of the Truman leadership in building a response to the challenge of Soviet power, the general trend of national policy continued to disturb many students of diplomacy. Some who accepted the need of Western rearmament rejected the customary definition of the Soviet danger employed to justify it. By mid-century it had become habitual for American officials to depict the Soviet problem in ideological rather than imperialistic terms. Former Ambassador to Russia Walter Bedell Smith, for example, warned the nation in June, 1949: "It is extremely important for the democracies, and especially the United States, never to lose sight of the fundamental fact that we are engaged in a constant, continuing, gruelling struggle for freedom and the American way of life that may extend over a period of many years."

Such observations on the Soviet threat properly recognized the unprecedented magnitude of the external challenge to Western security, but it was never made clear how this danger, if largely ideological, could be resolved by policies of military containment. To impose such obligations on American policy encumbered it with added burdens of fear and recalcitrance in a situation that under the best of conditions would have been difficult enough. For some frightened Americans who accepted the notion of limitless struggle, the world conflict, especially after the outbreak of the Korean War, had reached the state of intensity in which successful coexistence with the Soviet Union was no longer possible. One editor demanded that the President remove from his administration those "who have sold and fed him on the pap of 'co-existence' with Soviet Communism."

Kennan was among those who challenged the single-minded national concern with military strength, especially after the deepening of the military response with the North Korean aggression. To him the assumptions regard-

ing Soviet intentions and methods appeared to accept the
certainty of general war. If it was true that the Kremlin
was secretive and hostile, it had been that way since 1917.
If it overshadowed Europe with its armed might, it had
done so since 1945. The United States, he pointed out,
had coexisted with the U.S.S.R. for 33 years; it had no
choice but to do so in the future. If seemed doubtful,
moreover, if there was anything particularly new or sinis-
ter in the Soviet decision to use North Korean puppets in
the assault on South Korea. Few students of Russia believed Korea the beginning of another world war. Writing
in *The New York Times* of February 25, 1951, Kennan
accused those who condemned coexistence of assuming
that there were inexpensive means available for undoing
the power revolution of the previous decade. He reminded
them of the price their intolerance really advocated. "They
should not try," he said

> to comfort themselves and their readers with the flimsy
> pretense that this counsel of despair does not mean war.
> It does; and if this is the view they are going to take, let
> them have the forthrightness with themselves and with
> others to come out and say that what they are talking
> about is war and tell us how and to what ends and with
> what resources they propose we conduct that war, and
> how we are to assure the agreement of the members of a
> great coalition to a course founded on preconceptions
> which they do not share, and how a better world is sup-
> posed to emerge from the other end of this entire process.

Those who saw limited significance in the Korean War
questioned American policy toward Germany. The inclu-
sion of West Germany in the NATO treaty commitment,
warned James P. Warburg in May, 1949, would not only
involve the West in the rearming of Germany but would
also solidify the Eastern bloc. Nothing, he predicted,
would cement the Warsaw Pact alliance as the fear of a
rearmed Germany. To arm West Germany, warned Kennan, would create an unacceptable threat to the Soviet
Union and would divide Germany permanently into a
Western and Soviet sphere. Never, said the critics of German rearmament, would the Kremlin tolerate a united
Germany armed and free to pursue its own destiny. To
the British and French who accepted the need of rearming

Germany, American policy simply eliminated for them the necessity of facing the German problem at all.

Whatever the magnitude of its military structure, it was doubtful if the West could obtain a settlement with the U.S.S.R. on its own terms. To the extent that the new posture of strength vis-à-vis the Soviet Union had the limited purpose of containment it comprised a viable policy. But the persistent refusal of the Truman administration to define American objectives in terms other than self-determination placed the nation's goals beyond the capabilities of Western preparedness. American policy had been reduced to a package of means without ends. "Foreign policy in [Acheson's] regime," complained the Washington *Post* in April, 1951, "has become merely a carbon copy of Pentagon strategy without regard to policy or principle. A military man has to think in terms of war tomorrow, but not the diplomat."

Without some American willingness to accept the Russian gains of World War II there seemed to remain only the prospect of eventual war. One Washington *Post* editorial declared: "If it is assumed that every proposal coming from the other side is made in bad faith, then obviously no negotiation is possible. But negotiation is the essential business of diplomacy." Arthur M. Schlesinger, Jr., attacked what he regarded as a fundamental moralism in American foreign policy in the *Foreign Policy Bulletin* of February 23, 1951:

> . . . The policy of abstract moralism is an honorable and high-minded policy; but it is so concerned with being right in the abstract that it forgets to be effective. . . . The function of foreign policy is not to provide an outlet for moral indignation, however warranted that indignation may be. The function of foreign policy is to produce desired results.

European spokesmen, concerned with their region's security, lauded the vigorous leadership of Truman and Acheson is building the Western defense structure. But to Winston Churchill and British students of Russia it made considerable difference whether Western capacity was being designed to negotiate a suitable division of interests in Europe or to secure the unconditional surrender of the

Soviet Union. If successful negotiation was its purpose, then delay might be futile. Western power vis-à-vis Russia appeared as strong in 1950 as it was likely to become. Churchill argued for a negotiated settlement in January, 1948, in an address before the House of Commons:

> I will only venture to say that there seems to me to be very real danger in going on drifting too long. I believe that the best chance of preventing a war is to bring matters to a head and come to a settlement with the Soviet government before it is too late. This would imply that the Western democracies . . . would take the initiative in asking the Soviet for a settlement.

Two years later Churchill put his case before the House of Commons with even greater urgency. The Western position, he warned, was becoming weaker. "Therefore," he concluded, "while I believe there is time for further effort for a lasting and peaceful settlement, I cannot feel that it is necessarily a long time, or that its passage will progressively improve our own security. Above all things, we must not fritter it away."

But official Washington was not prepared, intellectually or politically, to follow such advice. The very notion of a global conflict in a fluid power structure rendered all diplomatic settlements illusive and meaningless. The limitless attacks on the Truman record, especially in the Far East, helped to solidify the American response in the cold war into a peculiarly American pattern. The administration's fundamental refusal to recognize the power revolution of the forties, either in Europe or Asia, carried with it an illusion of omnipotence which seemed to guarantee the ultimate victory of the West over its Communist enemies. Yet the nation could erect no force commensurate with the principles and pressures that determined its objectives abroad. It could neither settle its outstanding differences with Moscow or Peiping through diplomacy nor dispose of them through war. It could only drift along behind its moral principles while the persistent failure of those principles rendered them diplomatically impotent. Unable to employ either its power or its diplomacy, the nation could escape its diplomatic and intellectual dilemma only by assuming a world of unrelenting hostility in which diplomacy had no place.

— 4 —

SELF-DETERMINATION AND
EUROPEAN SECURITY

Russia's enduring hegemony over East-Central Europe comprised the central issue of the cold war. It was here that Stalin first challenged the illusion of Allied wartime unity when, in defiance of his wartime promises, he refused to relinquish Soviet control over the regions occupied by the Red Army in the closing months of World War II. Through the fifteen years which followed, the Soviet rulers resisted every Western effort to negotiate, in the name of self-determination of peoples, the diminution of Soviet military and political preponderance in the regions behind the Iron Curtain. Instead, the Kremlin pursued the antithetical goal of forcing the United States to agree to a division of Europe into two major spheres of influence, each nation guaranteeing the other primacy in its sphere. Together, ran the Soviet argument, the two super powers would prevent other nations from disturbing the equilibrium thus established. Premier Nikita Khrushchev phrased this Soviet expectation clearly in July, 1959: "We want to live in peace and friendship with Americans because we are the two most powerful countries and if we live in friendship these other countries will also live in friendship."

This Soviet vision of postwar Europe seemed wholly anachronistic. Its emphasis on naked power politics disturbed those who placed their hopes in the United Nations. The policies of repression appeared curiously out of place in an era when men and nations struggled successfully to be free. Indeed, Soviet conduct took its toll in the perennial defiance of national will and in the constant threat of rebellion. But if the political and military price which the maintenance of the Iron Curtain exacted of the U.S.S.R. was enormous, it did not strain the Soviet economy or modify Soviet purpose. This reality narrowed the alternatives for United States policy almost to the vanishing point.

From Containment to Liberation. Essentially, the U.S.S.R. gave the United States two realistic choices in Europe. Either this nation could bring overwhelming power to bear on the Soviet Union to force some compliance with the wartime agreements, or it could recognize the new Soviet hegemony and accept its existence as the basis of future negotiations. For American leadership, both Democratic and Republican, neither course was acceptable. Quite obviously the United States and its NATO Allies had no intention of destroying the Russian position in Eastern and Central Europe by force. On the other hand, they feared that any diplomatic recognition of Soviet aggression would appear to be an abandonment of clearly stated wartime principles and an admission that victory in 1945 had not ushered in a new era free from power politics. Strangely, the United States viewed the new Russian hegemony less as a threat to Western security than as a threat to Western ideals. It responded to the challenge of the Iron Curtain, not with power or diplomacy, but with an effort to escape the responsibilities of both. The resort to the rhetoric of disapprobation, so characteristic of American behavior throughout the fifties, often created the popular illusion of a vigorous policy vis-à-vis the Soviet Union whereas it actually served as a device to avoid the necessity of creating a policy at all.

Powerless to alter the status quo behind the Iron Curtain, the Truman administration sought to stabilize the line of military demarcation. To that end it employed American military and economic aid to rebuild the power of Western Europe and prevent further Russian encroachment on European soil. But this recognition of the Iron Curtain's existence was provisional, for American leaders assumed that successful containment would produce tensions within the Soviet structure and force modifications of Soviet purpose. Containment implied an eventual rollback of Soviet occupation. This ruled out the necessity of negotiating with the Soviet Union on the basis of spheres of influence in Europe.

When military containment soon demonstrated that it would not bring freedom automatically to the Iron Curtain countries, critics charged that the Truman policies merely relegated the captive peoples of Europe to permanent suppression. John Foster Dulles, who became Secretary of State in January, 1953, represented the burgeoning conviction that the United States could do better. He possessed a deep sense of the importance of moral force in international affairs and supreme confidence in the ultimate triumph of principle. In his article, "A Policy of Boldness," published in *Life*, May 19, 1952, he developed the concept that the nation had available moral resources that could topple the Soviet imperial structure. He cast aside the Truman-Acheson belief in limited power and long-range expectation as inadequate for the nation. Mr. Dulles charged that American policy was not even designed to win a conclusive victory in the cold war. It was conceived less to eliminate the Soviet peril than to live with it "presumably forever." The time had come, he wrote, to develop a *dynamic* foreign policy that conformed to *moral* principles. American policy must move beyond "containment"; it must anticipate the "liberation" of those who lived under compulsion behind the Iron Curtain. (*See Document No. 8.*)

Again in the Republican platform of 1952 Mr. Dulles promised a program that would "mark the end of the negative, futile and immoral policy of 'containment' which abandons countless human beings to a despotism and Godless terrorism which in turn enables the rulers to forge the captives into a weapon for our destruction." Mr. Dulles made clear his program as Secretary of State in an address before the Four-H Clubs Congress in November, 1954: "Liberation normally comes from within. But it is more apt to come from within if hope is constantly sustained from without. This we are doing in many ways." The concept of liberation demanded above all that the United States shun any settlement that would recognize Soviet control over alien peoples.

Unfortunately, the rhetoric of universal freedom created national goals based on aspirations that had no relation whatever to American power or American security interests. Because there was really no issue in Soviet-satellite relations that was vital to the United States, it was clear that any revolt behind the Iron Curtain could lead only to embarrassment. If the nation pressed its moral commitment to liberation, it might become involved in war. On the other hand, if in a crisis it denied its commitment, announced continually through a determined and anxious phraseology, the nation would demonstrate to the world that its pronouncements were meaningless as policy. The clear evidence that the declared purpose would not be backed by force would destroy even the diplomatic power of recognition.

Second, the national adherence to the goal of liberation, by permitting the United States to claim every challenge to the Soviet hegemony as a victory for American foreign policy, could only fasten the status quo more firmly on the satellites. It was doubtful if the Soviets would concede anything to the continuing pressures of nationalism if American officials heralded every concession as a Soviet admission of guilt. What was required were the means to permit the Russians to withdraw from the Iron Curtain without losing face. Certainly American policy could have no higher aim than to encourage the Russians to correct their own wrongs without appearing to be losing the game of diplomacy to the United States.

Third, the verbal commitment to liberation entailed a claim to guardianship which could involve the nation in war against its interests. As long as the United States identified itself openly with self-determination, the Soviets could well interpret any pressure against their control as the result of American interference. Should that pressure ever become acute enough to endanger Soviet security, American involvement, if only verbal, would endanger the peace of this nation. Governments must eventually bear the responsibility for their words as well as their actions.

The Challenge of Revolution.   Mr. Dulles faced his first test in 1956. For a decade the behavior of Communist dictatorships in Eastern Europe had produced currents of resistance. By the time of Stalin's death in 1953 it was obvious that the intense repression of the Soviet system was beginning to produce diminishing returns. Facing the liability of surly populations, the Khrushchev-Bulganin regime, confident of its strength, gambled on the proposition that it could secure greater allegiance to communism by easing the Soviet grip. In line with this conviction, Khrushchev in February, 1956, denounced the cult of leadership and stimulated the critical thought already released by the death of Stalin. Quickly the criticism encompassed the very structure of the Soviet system itself. There could be no limit to criticism once the principle that it could exist in any form had been established.

After the East Berlin riots of 1953, it was evident that the satellites were becoming restless under the new freedom. Everywhere there erupted a ferment of popular excitement, demanding better living conditions, a freer press, more representative government, and national independence similar to that enjoyed by Tito's Yugoslavia. In most nations local Communist leaders kept the new pressures within bounds by making concessions. In Poland the demand for changes quickly outran what the local regime could deliver. The result was the famed Poznan riots of June, 1956.

If such challenges to the Soviet monolith were the high purpose of American policy, it was essential that Washington not pour scorn and ridicule on the Kremlin because it appeared to be losing its grip on its own structure. When the tendency to chide developed in the summer of 1956, George F. Kennan pleaded in *Harper's*:

> Let us not, in particular, discourage evolution in this new direction by receiving it with wild boasts that it represents the triumph and vindication of our policies and the ignominious defeat for the Soviet leaders who have introduced these changes. The victories of democracy occur not when men are destroyed, but when they are illuminated and made wiser and more tolerant. If greater liberality now comes to the Soviet world, the victory belongs not to us but to the forces of health and hope that live— thank God—in men everywhere. . . . Let us have the humility to recognize these things, let us remember we are the agents, not the authors, of the eternal verities in which we profess to believe, and let us not take personal credit for what is in reality the power of these verities themselves.

When the rioting occurred in Poland, the United States government rightly disclaimed all responsibility. To the Poznan marchers American aspirations for liberation meant nothing. It was hunger and repression that drove them beyond desperation. In defying Poland's Communist regime they looked only to their own resources.

The Dilemma of Hungary.   But when the growing instability of the Soviet sphere produced the riots in Hungary, the United States became too deeply implicated to escape all responsibility. Secretary Dulles from the beginning identified American purpose with the aspirations of the revolting Hungarians. On October 27, 1956, he explained to the Dallas Council on World Affairs why this nation had taken the issue of Hungary to the U.N. Security Council. "These patriots," he said, "value liberty more than life itself. And all who peacefully enjoy liberty have a solemn duty to seek, by all truly helpful means, that those who now die for freedom will not have died in vain." He declared that the spirit of patriotism and the longing for freedom was at last breaking the Soviet grip on the lands behind the Iron Curtain. "The weakness of Soviet imperialism," the Secretary continued, "is being made manifest. Its weakness is not military weakness nor lack of material power. It is weak because it seeks to sustain an unnatural tyranny by suppressing human aspirations which cannot indefinitely be suppressed and by concealing truths which cannot indefinitely be hidden." Mr. Dulles invited the Hungarians, as they now achieved their independence, to draw upon the United States for aid in adjusting their economy to serve the needs of their own people.

Such boasts that the American-encouraged aspirations for freedom were now rending the Soviet hegemony asunder were drowned out within a week by the crash of Soviet tanks as they slowly ground down the revolutionary forces of Budapest. Some Hungarian leaders cried out for aid, assuming that this nation's purpose of liberation was more than a moral preachment. They were informed, with stark realism, that any American effort at assistance would precipitate World War III. In admitting at the moment of greatest urgency that Hungary's independence was not required by the security interests of the United States, American officials rendered the concept of liberation a mockery. Those who expected help from the West recalled in their bitterness the words of the American delegate at the U.N. declaring that the United States would never desert the people of Hungary. As one Budapest factory foreman said of Western broadcasts into Hungary, "The speakers in their studios in Munich had it easy: just talking, talking, talking. We did the fighting." One Hungarian at Eisenstadt spoke for many of his fellow refugees when he said, "After listening all these years to Radio Free Europe, we can never believe the West again." Hungary demonstrated that policy not guided by national interest becomes irresponsible when put to the test.

In its dilemma the United States turned to the U.N. The basic condemnatory resolution, introduced into the Security Council by the American delegate early on November 4, was eliminated by a Russian veto. Immediately the General Assembly was called into emergency session. That afternoon the Assembly passed the resolution, calling on the U.S.S.R. to stop its armed attack on the people of Hungary and to withdraw its forces from that nation without delay.

Prime Minister Nehru of India warned the West that condemnation would only intensify the conflict, for under moral pressure the Kremlin could not relent without some admission of immorality. As the U.N. passed resolution after resolution, the neutralist spokesmen of India, Indonesia, and Burma remained unalterably opposed to the Assembly's efforts to turn the Soviets out of Hungary with words. V. K. Krishna Menon of India declared realistically that it was "not possible, except by military intervention, to alter the course of affairs in Hungary, unless we bring into relationship of things, whatever authority, whatever government, exists in Hungary." To him the revolution was a matter to be negotiated between Hungary and the Soviet Union. U.N. interference would merely magnify the cold war between the United States and the U.S.S.R. without achieving any useful purpose. United States Ambassador Henry Cabot Lodge, observing that the neutralist nations were always the first to resist external interference when it applied to Asia, accused them of maintaining a double standard of international morality. That the U.N.

resolutions saved no Hungarians seemed to make no difference as long as the Soviet Union stood properly condemned.

By mid-December the Assembly had adopted ten resolutions rebuking the Russians for their actions in Hungary. What they had achieved for the defeated and disconsolate Hungarian rebels was not clear. In July, 1957, James J. Wadsworth, deputy United States delegate to the U.N., admitted sadly that the U.N. had not secured the freedom of the Hungarian people, but he found solace in the fact that the resolutions had mobilized the conscience of the world. "Never has a revolution been so widely known," he informed members of the American Bar Association in New York, "never has an oppression been so completely condemned. The fires of moral condemnation lighted at the U.N. are plaguing the Soviet rulers today and will continue to plague them for years to come."

The Futility of Liberation. American abstention in the Hungarian revolt demonstrated that even with the support of a major uprising this nation could not and would not change the 1945 line of demarcation. Yet Washington officials refused to accept even this lesson from the Hungarian debacle. American policy statements continued to condemn the Russians for their domination of Hungary. On the second anniversary of the Hungarian revolt the State Department announced: "These actions of the Soviet and Hungarian Government in defiance of the U.N. . . . have occasioned deep concern in the U.S. as elsewhere throughout the world. *They cannot and will not be ignored.*" In December, 1958, Ambassador Lodge declared at the U.N. that the Hungarian people "must be relieved of that scourge of terror. . . . If the existing tension is to be relaxed and the danger of still another tragic explosion ended, it will be necessary to end the injustice which causes the tension." After 1956 the U.N., under pressure from the United States, repeatedly called upon the Hungarian puppet regime to comply with the resolutions adopted so often and so overwhelmingly. But by 1960 the rapidly declining percentage of nations willing to engage in the annual censure of the U.S.S.R. looked less and less like an impressive moral judgment.

American declarations of indignation toward the Soviet posture in Eastern Europe perpetuated a utopian response to the challenge of Soviet behavior. Whereas they held out the promise of freedom, they scrupulously avoided any reference to means. They created the illusion that American moral purpose still comprised a substitute for containment, and encouraged Americans to forget that in their purpose of freeing the satellites it was not their relations with Eastern Europe that mattered, but their relations with the Soviet Union. What the verbal adherence to liberation could achieve other than the continued disillusionment of those who took it seriously was not apparent. And yet if no one took it seriously, the rhetoric of freedom had no purpose at all.

In its failure to control events behind the Iron Curtain, the United States eventually conceded everything but principle. Yet in refusing to concede principle, the nation admitted only its unwillingness to act under the conditions which existed. The continuing appeal to principle conveyed the warning that the nation might, under altered circumstances, attempt to undo what it had not accepted. It was for this reason that the decision to sustain a perennial rebuke toward a situation of power entailed a vast danger, for in a crisis an impatient and fearful Russia might give the United States the clear-cut and sudden choice between principle and war, just as did the Japanese in 1941. When a nation's goals, anchored to aspirations, encompass more than its interests, it must in a crisis either fight for what is less than vital or beat an ignominious retreat. Neither reaction can serve the true interests of the nation.

The Conflict Over Germany. Germany presented the second stubborn problem in Soviet-American relations. Whereas the disposal of this issue, like that of Eastern Europe, remained firmly in Soviet hands, the Kremlin was forced to assume a more costly and uncontrollable commitment in its German policies than elsewhere within the Soviet sphere. For here it defied the will not only of the 17 million Germans under its control, but also of the 52 million that resided outside its hegemony. It was the Soviet Union alone that paid the price of maintaining the division of Germany and of sustaining the Allied wartime objective of curtailing the military power of the defeated nation.

For the Soviets the price was not too high, for control of East Germany was the keystone of the entire Soviet structure. Even the tenuous Soviet proposals for unification insisted on a German confederation which would leave the political status of East Germany unaltered. To Russians over thirty the Nazi invasion of June, 1941, was still the most significant date in their memory; Russians much younger could recall the thousands of destroyed cities, towns, and villages that bore mute testimony after 1945 of the violence of the German invasion. If Russia's own postwar development and its military establishment removed the immediate danger of another German invasion, there existed in Russia the fear that Germany, to gain its national objectives, might embroil the Western powers in a war against the Soviet Union. A united and free Germany, moreover, would endanger the entire Communist structure of Poland and Czechoslovakia. The central purpose of Soviet foreign policy was to prevent the destruction or subversion of the Russian hegemony by German power.

Nor was the U.S.S.R. alone in its fear and resentment of the rebuilding of Germany's military establishment. The Czechs and Poles especially had not forgotten the bestiality of the Nazi occupation and regarded every new German division as a potential force for Irredentism. By the late fifties Eastern European intellectuals pointed to the fact that Germany was again printing atlases which showed part of Czechoslovakia and Poland as belonging legitimately to a unified Germany. For them the thought of an armed and aggressive Germany held more terrors than did postwar Russia.

American policy simply denied the legitimacy of Soviet efforts to curb German power, through the forced division of the country, as another infringement on the principle of self-determination. In applying this principle to Germany, the United States demanded nothing less than unification under free elections. Any concession to the Soviets, ran the standard American argument, would result in the acceptance of either a divided Germany or conditions that would expose West Germany to Soviet encroachment. American purpose for Germany was synonymous with its purpose for the satellites. It sought the dismantling of the Soviet sphere in Europe by demanding the fulfillment of Russia's wartime promises, unmindful of the fact that such a proposal asked Moscow to abandon all the advantages that nation had won by its close-run victory in World War II. It would, in effect, transform the enemy of the United States in that war into the victor, the major ally into the loser. American purpose, in short, demanded that the Soviets agree to the maintenance of an opposing alliance which included not only their wartime allies, but their wartime enemies as well. It was not strange that the Russians never took the Western proposals seriously.

American objectives in Germany appeared so eminently satisfactory because they combined this nation's principles with its interests, for both would be served by a Soviet retreat to its boundaries of 1939. Yet the American preference for the triumph of German over Russian will appeared less the result of a studied evaluation of Western interests than the result of an immediate ambition to undermine the postwar position of the Soviet Union. Russia's perennial fear of Germany had always given its policies toward that country a certain consistency. American policy toward Germany moved in twenty years from militant neutrality to intense enmity to undisguised approbation. Indeed, after 1950 the villain of 1945 could do no wrong. The effort to contain Russia, in large measure, with German power was reminiscent of the Western diplomacy toward Hitler that came crashing to the ground with the Nazi-Soviet Pact of 1939 and Hitler's subsequent attack on the West. Western diplomacy tended to resurrect the hope of the thirties—that an armed and united Germany would somehow resolve the Russian problem. It was not clear that such a policy would serve the West any better in the future than it had in the past.

Both to prevent the Soviets from stabilizing the division of Germany and to sustain the German sense of unity, the Western powers recognized only the Western Federal Republic. Even the U.S.S.R. exchanged diplomatic representatives with the Bonn government; the importance of West Germany in European affairs gave it no logical alternative. Chancellor Conrad Adenauer of West Germany

made the denial of legitimacy to the puppet government
of East Germany a cardinal policy, convinced that any
recognition of that regime by the West would undermine
his own government and lead to a permanent division of
his country. So strongly was the government at Bonn opposed to recognition that it broke off diplomatic relations
with Yugoslavia when Tito offered diplomatic recognition
to East Germany.

Western Europe's Attachment to the Status Quo.
This nation's perennial failure to undermine the Soviet
hegemony did not destroy the popularity of its policies in
Western Europe. It was not that Europe's conservative
spokesmen had any interest in this nation's moral purpose
of liberating Eastern Europe. As one European diplomat,
after praising American cooperation in saving the Western coalition, remarked at the London Conference in
September, 1954: "This is fine, we will accomplish what
we came here for; but please, let us not try to do more,
let us not embark on any American 'paper' to turn the
Russians out of Poland." What mattered to Western Europe was the determination of the administration of President Dwight D. Eisenhower to perpetuate the Truman
policy of military containment. To Allied leaders containment was always a viable and laudable objective, for they
never expected more of American power than the maintenance of the status quo of 1945.

For many Europeans the division of the continent into
two huge military camps was their guarantee against uncertainty. Despite their words to the contrary, they
doubted the wisdom of any diplomatic settlement which
would achieve a united Germany with a will of its own.
Countless numbers of Western Europeans had no intention of facing a powerful, free, and ambitious Germany
again. They, like the Russians, would regard its creation
as the final measure of their defeat in World War II.
Rather than face such a hazard, they accepted willingly
policies which, because they demanded too much, had the
effect of perpetuating a divided Europe, guaranteed in its
stability by American and Soviet forces. Even few West
German leaders believed that unification was vital enough
to pursue on any terms which the Soviets might accept.
Western conservatives had no greater desire to replace

oppression with instability in Eastern Europe. Before their
submergence into the Nazi empire in 1939 and 1940, these
nations were neither orderly nor democratic. With the exception of Czechoslovakia, they were weak, authoritarian,
without balanced economies, and torn by minority problems. They could not manage their internal affairs or play
any reassuring role in world politics. If Soviet occupation
defied the principle of self-determination, it at least eliminated one dangerous aspect of the perennial German-
Russian conflict. As independent nations lying between a
rejuvenated Germany and a security-conscious Russia, the
Slavic states would again invite aggression and war as
they did in 1939.

Many Europeans regarded the status quo too acceptable
to be endangered with change. They believed that the hard
military line, symbolizing a divided Europe, was the continent's best guarantee of peace. No nation could challenge
it without the deliberate intention of starting a war. Since
the military stalemate was the best of all achievable worlds,
any policy that endangered Western security in pursuit of
a German settlement or an ephemeral new deal for the
satellites would be, in their estimation, utterly irrational.
As Alan Bullock, Censor of St. Catherine's Society, Ox-
ford, declared in 1958: "However much, and however
sincerely, we may wring our hands, we are not going to
endanger the status quo in order to help the peoples on
the other side of the Iron Curtain. The fact that Europe
is divided, and Germany too, it no doubt deplorable, but
I do not believe that this fact by itself will lead to a disturbance of the status quo."

This widespread devotion to the stability afforded by a
militarily divided Europe separated Western interests almost imperceptibly from those of the U.S.S.R. That this
broad area of agreement was not reflected in Western
diplomacy resulted partially from West German intransigence, partially from a general disinclination to concede
the principle of self-determination. Any diplomatic acceptance of the division of Europe would force the West
to share with the Kremlin the responsibility for thwarting
German and East European nationalism. By defending
principle, the West tied German interests to NATO and
placed the onus of repression squarely on the Soviets.

What the West gained, in short, by denying the legitimacy of Soviet action, was the force which nationalism could exert on the Soviet structure.

Unfortunately, this advantage had real meaning only in the context of a determined Western effort to unite Germany and free the captive nations—a purpose that did not exist in Western policy at any time after 1945. The West had no more interest in the resurgence of German or Slavic nationalism than did the Soviet Union. Every expression of self-determination within the Soviet sphere would be as much an embarrassment to the West as a danger to the U.S.S.R. The identification of Western interest with German and East European nationalism—supposedly the principal assurance of the West's ultimate triumph over Soviet repression—was a relationship that would be denied in any crisis.

Nationalism could endanger the Soviet structure only at the price of war. For that reason Western policy could fulfill its purpose for the captive nations only to the extent that it preserved their environment from anarchy and destruction. It could not serve the oppressed before it had established better and more relaxed relations with the Kremlin, for the evolution of the satellites toward freedom—and Germany toward unification—could result only from an increase in Soviet security. It was ironic that the West's verbal devotion to self-determination, because it was inimical to Soviet security interests, was the chief guarantee that self-determination would have little chance of success. Whatever the verbal assault on the Iron Curtain, it was so meaningless within the context of European politics, and yet so dangerous in its ultimate implications, that the West's fundamental policies were forced to accept either the status quo or war.

The Problem of West Berlin. Successful as the Kremlin leaders had been in forcing a practical acceptance of the status quo on the West, they could not view past stability as the fulfillment of Soviet diplomacy. They could neither relax nor enjoy their advantage as long as the Russian hegemony defied even the aspirations of Germany and much of the West. Ultimate Soviet security required Western recognition of a divided Europe, for this alone would commit the West as well as the U.S.S.R. to the limitation of Germany authority. To force this concession from the West, the Soviets attempted again after 1958 to exploit Western vulnerability at its exposed outpost of West Berlin.

Actually West Berlin's status threatened Soviet security as well. This city of 2.2 million West Germans, garrisoned by token forces from the West in accordance with wartime agreements, and located a hundred miles east of the Iron Curtain, prevented the consolidation of the Soviet hegemony. Its symbolism as the capital of a united Germany impeded the crystallization of the concept of two Germanies. West Berlin, moreover, was an escape hatch through which thousands of East Germans escaped— many of them valuable citizens—to the West. Even West Berlin's prosperity was a source of embarrassment for the Kremlin. During the fifties the city sprouted handsome buildings, elegant shops, and obvious comforts. Nowhere was the contrast between the progress of West Germany and the slow and painful development of the unwieldy East German economy more apparent. West Berlin, with the easy atmosphere of free minds, demonstrated the achievements of a free economy and refuted in a thousand ways the Communist theories of Western stagnation and decay. As a showcase of freedom and prosperity, the city was a constant irritant to the Soviets and a source of discontent to the East German and satellite peoples. Yet its chief significance in European diplomacy lay in the fact that it was a point at which the Soviets could apply pressure to secure what was fundamental to their purpose— the recognition of a divided Germany.

In November, 1958, Premier Khrushchev touched off a crisis when he challenged the Allied status in West Berlin in a note to the Western powers:

> The Soviet Government has resolved . . . to abolish the occupation regime in Berlin. . . . At the same time the Soviet Government is ready to open negotiations with [the West] on granting West Berlin the status of a demilitarized free city. . . . It is obvious that some time is needed. . . . In view of this, the Soviet Government proposes to make no changes in the present procedure for military traffic [to West Berlin] for half a year. . . . If the above period is not used for reaching a relevant agree-

ment, the Soviet Union will effect the planned measures
by agreement with the German Democratic Republic.

Russia, said Khrushchev, was willing to have the U.N.
share "in observing the free-city status of West Berlin."
He assured the West that he had no intention of com-
munizing the city. But his warning was clear. Either the
West would accept his program or the U.S.S.R. would
sign a separate peace treaty with the East German regime
and give it control of the access routes into West Berlin.

During the Geneva Conference of Foreign Ministers,
which convened in May, 1959, to consider the Berlin
question, the Western powers refused to concede their
legal rights of access to West Berlin. Having pledged
themselves to the defense of the city's inhabitants, they
could agree to no compromise that might infringe upon
their responsibility for the status of the free Berliners. Nor
would they recognize the East German regime. Dean
Acheson wondered why the Western powers consented to
negotiate at all. The Western position in Berlin, he said,
was quite satisfactory.

Throughout the Geneva deliberations, which again
turned on the fundamental question of Germany's future,
the Western position reflected its devotion to the principle
of self-determination. Andrei Gromyko, representing the
Soviet Union, based his position on power rather than
principle. He denied the validity of self-determination for
Germany. He recalled repeatedly what Hitler's Germany
had done to Europe when it enjoyed self-determination.
The total failure of the negotiations at Geneva, which
terminated finally in August, illustrated the crucial importance of Berlin and Germany to the continuing struggle
in Europe. In the basic conflict between Western principle and Soviet security interests lay the continuing cold
war.

That the West moved through the Berlin crisis of 1959-
1960 without either conceding anything or preparing for
any action simply reflected the status of big power diplomacy in the postwar world. Behind the mutual restraint
in action, if not in rhetoric, was the fundamental caution
encouraged by the nuclear capability on each side. Second,
the continued absence of armed conflict suggested that the
unresolved issues between East and West were consider-

ably less than vital. The stability of Europe reflected the realization among Western and Soviet leaders that the issues of the cold war were better left unresolved than disposed of by war. Third, behind the continuing lack of diplomatic settlement lay the notion, held equally by Americans and Soviets, that time was on their side. For some the avoidance of serious negotiations was the surest guarantee that world politics would some day square with their own purpose. The crisis would come when one side discovered that it had expected too much of time. It was then that the world would produce statesmanship of the highest order or pay the consequences of drift.

To recognize the East German government for an equivalent benefit would comprise a serious affront to German nationalism, but it would not infringe on any vital interest of the Western world. Indeed, by 1960 the West had coexisted with the East German regime quite satisfactorily for fifteen years. American interests, moreover, were not identical with those of Germany. Germany's national objectives required the total exclusion of Soviet interests from Central Europe; those of England, France, and the United States did not. This nation had no obligation to pursue the illusion of German unification under free elections merely to satisfy German nationalists, especially when such purpose required a Soviet capitulation. Every Russian government since Peter the Great had asserted its primary interest in Central Europe and had been willing to fight for it. Quite obviously European diplomacy would remain barren until it began to balance the interests of Germany with those of all the wartime Allies. The status quo—the only point of commencement available—had served the interests of the Western powers, including West Germany, quite as much as it had the Soviet Union.

Europe's Unresolved Problems. Through fifteen postwar years the containment policies of the United States had stabilized a divided Europe. This fundamental arrangement, supported by mutual, if unacknowledged, interests and a military stalemate, left all of Europe's long-term challenges unresolved. Statesmen and scholars were still concerned with the evolution of the continent toward some new condition which better represented the national aspirations of all captive peoples. If Europe's political structure was stable, it was obviously not permanent. In Lincoln's phaseology, Europe could not remain indefinitely half slave and half free. Yet how could Europe cease to be divided without stumbling into war? The West's vast military establishment had served only one purpose— to guarantee security in a divided continent. It had, in fact, accentuated the division of Europe. Yet many Western spokesmen warned that any diminution of that power on the Continent would bring the Soviet forces down on Western Europe. Europe's evolution, whatever the problem of security, still required the disintegration of the Iron Curtain. Unless Western power could contribute to this end, it assured nothing but the continued separation of the Continent into two spheres of influence.

German nationalism continued to threaten the Iron Curtain and with it the peace of the world. As Secretary of State Christian A. Herter warned the Soviets at Geneva in May, 1959: "It is the teaching of history that the artificial partition of a strong and vigorous people can only result in disaster for those that stand in the way of their reunification. Only the whole German people can be entrusted with the task of determining the future of the German nation. Until the Soviet Union recognizes these self-evident facts and cooperates to this end, there will never be a solution of the German problem or the problem of European security." For the West the danger lay not only in the possibility that resurgence of German nationalism might lead to war, but also in the fact that Germany, in its disillusionment with Western policy, might one day negotiate unilaterally with the Kremlin to achieve unification.

Even the satellites were consigned by Soviet repression to an anomalous position. They were neither independent states nor blocks in the Soviet structure. Time could only free them or destroy their national entities. There was danger that continued repression would create a general apathy and despair which would undermine all national ambition. The failure of Western diplomacy to mitigate Soviet retaliation in Hungary read a powerful lecture to the satellite peoples. In retrospect it was clear that the simple Western appeal to self-determination had been a device for avoiding rather than facing the hard problems posed by the captive nations.

Disengagement. Such fundamental and unanswered questions as these gave rise in the late fifties to the burgeoning concept of "disengagement." George F. Kennan first gave it form and synthesis in his Reith Lectures over the BBC in the late autumn of 1957, later published under the title of *Russia, the Atom, and the West*. Kennan accepted the traditional goals of Western diplomacy—the achievement of greater self-determination for the captive peoples, including those of East Germany. Any evolution toward self-determination, he pointed out, required nothing less than the voluntary withdrawal of Soviet occupation forces from the Iron Curtain countries. But since the question of Soviet occupation could not be divorced from that of Russian security, he suggested that NATO also disengage its forces from West Germany and agree to the neutralization of that nation. Lastly, he recommended the establishment of a nuclear-free band across Central Europe, an idea popularized in January, 1958, by Adam Rapacki, the Foreign Minister of Poland. Disengagement, in short, questioned the fundamental decisions of the past which had assumed that desired changes within the Soviet sphere could best be achieved by perpetuating a hard military line of demarcation across Europe.

Kennan doubted that the withdrawal of NATO forces from Germany and the elimination of that country from the alliance would endanger Western security. If the Soviets reoccupied the vacuum created by mutual agreement or even attacked the West, NATO could respond as quickly and successfully as any other arrangement would permit, for nuclear power had long comprised the West's basic defense structure. Kennan's impact on European liberals was profound. The German Social Democrats immediately came up with a phased program of their own. Indeed, they advised the Bonn government to negotiate unilaterally with the U.S.S.R., charging that the West had nothing to offer but more intransigence.

Dean Acheson's sweeping criticism of Kennan's thesis appeared in *Foreign Affairs*, April, 1958. His arguments reaffirmed NATO's traditional commitment to military containment. He doubted that the West could ever pay the requisite price for a Soviet military retreat without weakening its own security, for the Kremlin had consistently demanded the liquidation of NATO.

European conservatives had a deep commitment to NATO, for security held top priority in their scale of values. They regarded the Atlantic Alliance as the primary achievement of postwar diplomacy, and attributed the amazing economic recovery of Western Europe to its existence. Thus they opposed any change in its structure. To them the Rapacki Plan for a nuclear-free zone was nothing less than a Soviet trap. Second, they feared that any withdrawal of Allied forces from Germany would terminate in the complete elimination of American troops from Europe. "It would be folly," declared Paul-Henri Spaak, Secretary General of NATO, in June, 1959, "and I venture to say criminal folly, to follow a policy which might lead to the departure of American troops from Germany." Disengagement would eventually remove the United States, the keystone of Western security, from the European scene, warned Spaak, and reëstablish the conditions that led to war in the thirties. Third, the neutralization of Germany, ran the conservative argument, would withdraw German forces and space from NATO, curtail the alliance's effectiveness, and forever limit its operations to nuclear weapons. "Deadlock and stalemate are certainly hard to endure," admitted one British official, "but to yield would be worse. We should all of us do well not to forget that lesson of the nineteen-thirties."

Acheson challenged the notion that the U.S.S.R. could afford to evacuate the satellites as part of an agreement on disengagement. Retiring Soviet forces would leave in their wake a group of unstable Communist regimes whose collapse the Kremlin could not tolerate without risking the overthrow of its entire system. It was equally improbable, Acheson wrote, that the Soviets would accede to the absorption of East Germany into the economy and political structure of West Germany. Such an eventuality, he warned, would bring the Soviets back into Central Europe in force.

Lastly, Acheson, ever mindful of the basic American purpose of breaking up the Iron Curtain, found the means for achieving this objective in NATO itself. A powerful and united Western Europe, he wrote, exerted a radiating influence on the Soviet sphere. It had prevented the total repression of Poland and Yugoslavia; in time it would subvert the entire Soviet structure. A thriving Western economy would produce vast economic change behind the Iron Curtain. How this would affect the political structure of the Soviet sphere he explained in *Foreign Affairs*:

> With the rise in the standard of living in the Soviet Union, and as some broader participation in the direction of affairs was made essential by their very magnitude and complexity, the Russian need for forced communization and iron control of Eastern Europe would diminish. Then negotiations, looking toward a united Germany, under honorable and healing conditions and toward the return of national identity to the countries of Eastern Europe while preserving also the interests of the Russian people in their own security and welfare, could for the first time be meaningful and show buds of hope.

Containment and Deadlock. Containment remained a program of sanguine expectation. For its creators, its mission had not changed. It would not only prevent Soviet expansion, but would eventually produce the long-desired changes within the Soviet sphere. In contrast to the concept of disengagement, military containment promised the ultimate triumph of self-determination without any loss of security or without the need of recognizing Soviet interests in Eastern and Central Europe. It promised a triumph of German over Russian purpose without war. The continuing arms race was merely the price required for security. It was the assurance that the play for time would result in self-determination before it would result in open conflict. Unfortunately, the quiet anticipation of change avoided the central issue of European politics—the future of Russo-German relations. The Soviet hegemony was, in large measure, the Kremlin's answer to a problem born of long and painful experience. That East Germany was the keystone of the postwar Soviet political structure suggested an immutable purpose. How time alone could resolve the German question without benefit of serious diplomacy was nowhere in evidence.

This nation's response to the Iron Curtain was characterized during the fifties by a disturbing dichotomy. Its policies of containment, brilliantly conceived to counter the threat of Soviet imperialism, revealed the power to stabilize a divided Europe. They never revealed the power to do more. This fact alone established the limits of successful national action. It is difficult to see how the United States could have achieved more vis-à-vis the Soviet Union in Europe before 1960 than it did. But Secretary Dulles, having promised the liberation of the captive peoples, not through the quiet passage of time, but through the application of moral principles, became imprisoned by the public opinion he helped to create. He could not achieve what he had promised; domestic pressures would not permit him to accept less. In this self-imposed dilemma he could sustain his personal popularity before Congress and the nation only by placing the blame for his failure on Soviet intransigence. This reduced his conduct of foreign policy to a futile incantation of principles that had no relationship to Europe's power structure. It subordinated American diplomacy to the requirements of domestic politics.

Eventually such meaningless and inconsistent behavior exacted its price on the country. Dulles admitted readily that it left no room for diplomatic maneuvering. "We must avoid war," he said, "and still stand firm and affirmative for what we deem to be just and right." When a nation treads such a narrow course, two questions are always pertinent: Is the course demanded by the national interest? Does it bring rewards commensurate with the dangers being courted? In Europe Dulles' achievements, other than the continued containment of the Soviet sphere which was in no way anchored to his perennial condemnation of Soviet repression, were negligible. But his refusal to concede any legitimacy to the Soviet quest for security, while it gained nothing, transformed every American demand to the high realm of unshakable purpose. It kept the American people on a war footing emotionally, if not militarily. It did not prepare them to accept the only kind of peace available to them. Herein lay the deep tragedy of the concept of liberation. It taught the American people to expect through peaceful means what they could actually have only through war. It created a dangerous habit of mind which could chain American leadership to the everlasting and futile pursuit of the unachievable.

Any break in the European deadlock required both a retreat from principle and a retreat from the heavy reliance on the arms race. Both requirements involved risks but not trust of the Soviet Union. Trust has no legitimate place in diplomacy, for nations have neither soul nor conscience. The essential purpose of diplomacy has always been to discover and adjust conflicting interests. That the mutual interests of East and West in Europe were legion was obvious from the continent's very stability. What European peace demanded above all was the diplomatic recognition of those national commitments which could be infringed upon only at the price of war. By definition, this conceded only what was vital to the opposition. Successful peacetime negotiations had never done less. Whatever arrangements were claimed by the Soviets were already supported by ample military power. The United States could hardly give away what it did not have.

Even the decision to anchor diplomacy to the task of balancing Soviet and Western interests in Europe was no assurance of satisfactory negotiations. There remained the persistent obstacle of Soviet deviousness and misunderstanding of the West. But the Kremlin's rejection of a reasonable proposal for a settlement in Central Europe would place the onus of diplomatic stalemate on that nation for the first time in the cold war. Sound and concrete proposals would undermine the Soviet peace crusade throughout the free world. Any consistent Soviet reaction to serious Western proposals which genuinely recognized Russia's security interests would establish as had nothing in the decade of the fifties the true nature of Soviet imperialism—whether it sought to stabilize or upset the status quo. Thereafter, whatever the Russian behavior, there would be little excuse for the conviction that a policy of drift which prepared the nation neither for war nor for peace was in itself successful policy. For what really mattered in Western security was as much Western determination as Soviet intent. Western morale could not be sustained unless people facing the constant threat of atomic annihilation could live under the conviction that Western leadership had neglected no avenue to peace.

— 5 →

THE CHALLENGE OF CHANGE

Like Caesar's Gaul, the world is divided into three parts. That this was not obvious in the immediate postwar years was attributable to the dominance of the Soviet-Western conflict in international affairs. World War II had witnessed the rise of two super powers on the ashes of five other great nations that had been badly weakened by the demands of unconditional surrender—England, France, Italy, Germany, and Japan. With the establishment of the Soviet hegemony in Eastern Europe, a bipolar world replaced the traditional world of multiplicity and constantly shifting alignments. The United States and the U.S.S.R., like two huge magnets amid crumbling military structures, pulled the key nations of Europe like steel filings toward the poles. Those countries which continued to hover in orbits of their own were unimportant individually and collectively. The vast Afro-Asian world, still tied in large measure to Europe's faltering empires, played no active or recognizable role in international affairs.

The Challenge of Nationalism. As Europe moved toward a new stability, enforced by unprecedented peacetime military establishments, Asia and Africa unleashed another disquieting cold war on the world—a war against their own colonial past. This struggle had no relationship to the conflict in Europe, for it rested on foundations slowly formed since the dawn of the century. This awakening of the vast underdeveloped continents, which would eventually revolutionize world politics and counter all postwar tendencies toward bipolarism, resulted initially from the dichotomy, growing throughout the century, between the wealth, education, and intelligence of foreign-trained native elites and their subordinate political and racial status imposed by a history of colonial and white rule. These leaders, in their struggle for recognition and power, searched for those popular appeals which might excite in their backward populations the fundamentally European emotion of nationalism. This emotion they could then employ in the name of the masses to strengthen their onslaught on the old order, whether that order were identified with European colonialism or indigenous feudalism. Always the new nationalism was anchored ideologically to three essential principles of Western civilization—racial equality, self-determination of peoples, and social justice. As late as World War II native leaders had achieved little against the reluctance of the Western powers to part with their imperial structures.

Japan's successful invasion of Southeast Asia in 1941 and 1942 instilled new courage in native nationalists and brought the underlying revolution to a new stage of insistence. As one Malay leader declared, "Yes, I worked for the Japanese during the war. They did more to awaken my country than all the years of English rule. They showed us what Asians could accomplish." One month after the fall of Singapore the astute London *Economist* warned: "There can be no return to the old system once Japan has been defeated. . . . The need is for entirely new principles or rather the consistent application of principles to which lip service has long been paid." Asian leaders warned the West that the settlements following the war would embody the concept of Asiatic equality or there would be no security for the West in the Orient; any white armies on Asian soil fighting to maintain the status quo against native forces, whatever the justice of their cause, would be regarded *ipso facto* as the aggressors.

After 1945 the old empires, now subjected to unprecedented pressures, began to disintegrate. The colonial powers, exhausted by war and encouraged by the United States, conceded to the inevitable. Through an orderly transition the regions of South and Southeast Asia under British and Dutch rule achieved self-determination. In Indochina French intransigence quickly involved that dying empire in a costly and futile civil war. Within a half dozen years over 600 million people had achieved their independence; over a billion Asians had changed their form of government, expelling regimes that had appeared unshakable when war came to Asia in 1941.

But the revolutionary pressures against the status quo were merely gaining momentum as the emotions which they unleashed threatened to tear down every imperial vestige of the past. Increasingly millions of Asians and Africans discovered, through modern instantaneous communication, that elsewhere the world had undergone fantastic improvements in living standards. The pervading conviction that their own poverty and backwardness had been imposed by misrule stimulated the so-called "revolution of rising expectations." No government, whatever its nature, could ignore it with impunity. As the demands of self-determination gripped the more poverty-stricken and autocratically-governed regions of Asia, the Middle East, and Africa, the voices of native leaders became more strident and hysterical in their demands for change. In Africa the jungle backwardness of black populations emphasized the question of racial inequality and led Premier Nkrumah of Ghana to observe, "There will be no peace until the world has learned to put its relations with Africa and the man of color on a new basis of freedom, equality, mutual respect and dignity."

The New Nations in World Affairs. In a world of unprecedented ideological conflict, Asian and African nationalism was neither right nor left. As an indigenous movement, its leadership and intent were molded largely by local conditions. For Afro-Asian nationalists, therefore, Western political and economic organization had limited appeal. Their distinction as national heroes permitted no significant political or military concessions to foreign powers. Nor was their perennial resort to violence any evidence of Communist or Fascist indoctrination. If they preached dogma and discipline, it was because in a non-democratic order the road to power was revolution, not the ballot. Communist success, wherever it occurred, resulted from the ability of its leaders to capture the mood and the program of the nationalists.

What the new nations required was time and opportunity to establish themselves as viable political and economic entities. Such ambitions motivated them against involvement in world politics. But sophisticated national leaders quickly discovered that the United Nations gave their countries a voice in international affairs completely disproportionate to their power and responsibilities. As the Afro-Asian nations swelled the U.N. membership in the late fifties, they played an increasingly important role in the organization's activities.

At the U.N., as in all their foreign activities, the new nations stood firm on the issues that affected them; toward those that divided the world they remained uncommitted. First, they were determined to defend their individual sovereignties. President Sukarno of Indonesia reminded a joint session of Congress in May, 1956, that whatever the aid which Asians received from others, they would permit no material advantage to buy from them any part of their hard-won freedom. In their foreign policies the Afro-Asian nations would settle for nothing less than eventual self-determination for their continents. As Sukarno declared before a New York audience during his 1956 tour of the United States, "In this age, the age of Asian and African nationalism, there can be no final peace or security until the last vestiges of colonialism have been swept into the ash can of history along with Fascism, feudalism, slavery, and other rubbish of the ages. . . ."

Second, the new nations defended repeatedly their right to remain aloof from the East-West struggle. As early as October, 1949, in an address at Columbia University, Nehru of India outlined the program of neutralism, "The main objectives of that policy are: the pursuit of peace, not through alignment with any major power or group of powers, but through an independent approach to each controversial or disputed issue. . . ." Since official doctrine of the neutralist nations regarded both power blocs responsible for the cold war in Europe, to join either one would endanger the interests and the self-respect of the new sovereignties. Nehru observed at Bandung in April, 1955, that it was "an intolerable humiliation for any nation of Asia or Africa to degrade itself by becoming a camp follower of one or the other of the power blocs. . . ." For many neutralists this refusal to take sides became an end in itself. One African diplomat remarked at the 1960 session of the U.N. General Assembly: "Neither side has won us, and we are determined that neither will."

The Soviet Response. This fundamental instability of the non-European world produced a clear dichotomy in Soviet purpose abroad. In Europe Russia had a vested interest in stability. Any war in Europe would erase the achievements of the past and terminate the slow and painful evolution of Soviet society toward its goal of peace and plenty. Increasingly the Russian emphasis on coexistence revealed a deep commitment to the European status quo. Communism was the means by which Moscow maintained control of its satellite empire. Almost totally removed from that ideology was the Russian nation itself, pursuing historic objectives of national interest vis-à-vis the powers of Western Europe.

But outside the Western World the U.S.S.R. identified its interests with turbulence and change. Soviet leaders, the product of revolution themselves, accepted without equivocation the basic tendencies of the age. They saw as early as World War I that the arrogant and tranquil world, erected and maintained by the superior power and organization of Western Europe, was growing increasingly unstable. V. I. Lenin, the founder of the Soviet state, declared in 1921 that the "millions and hundreds of millions [of the colonial countries] . . . are now coming forward as independent, active, revolutionary factors. It is perfectly clear that in the impending decisive battles in the world revolution, the movement of the majority of the population of the globe, which is first directed towards national liberation, will turn against capitalism and will, perhaps, play a much more revolutionary part than we expect." After World War II the revolutionary fervor, anticipated a quarter century earlier by Lenin, could no longer be contained. All that remained for Soviet leaders was to scavenge it—to stimulate it, guide it, and exploit it.

Soviet advantage in a revolutionary world was apparent everywhere. If the older imperial world belonged to Western Europe alone, the Russians had only to identify themselves with the anti-Western forces to capture some of the West's lost prestige. Always they sought to provide aspiring societies with alternative concepts and methods for achieving their goals. The U.S.S.R. had demonstrated that a nation could build its economy through controlled production and consumption rather than awaiting the slow accumulation of capital through the profits of free enterprise. The Soviet system accepted the sacrifice of life and comfort, even tyranny, as the price of material progress. It emphasized cooperation and national purpose rather than individual wealth and individual freedom. The Communist way presented a model to nations in a hurry, motivated by an awakening national consciousness, but with insufficient resources to permit capital accumulation through private economic activity alone. Unfortunately for the West, in much of the Afro-Asian world the fundamental attributes of Western civilization were irrelevant, for it was not clear how either democracy or capitalism could take root in that environment. Individual freedom often seemed less essential than collective freedom from alien rule. The Soviet emphasis on national achievement rather than individual rights, on efficiency rather than democracy, gave the Soviet system a pertinence which the Western example did not have.

To expand Soviet influence and to carry the ideological conflict into the underdeveloped continents, the Russian leaders moved into most revolutionary situations of the fifties, peddling goods and offering money, markets, advice, and even guns. After 1956 the U.S.S.R. invaded the field of foreign aid and quickly expanded its piecemeal beginnings into a grand strategy. The Soviet economy appeared capable of sustaining an ever-widening scale of activity abroad. In their effort to penetrate the former Western hegemony through policies of trade and aid, the Soviets possessed several clear advantages. Russia, unlike the United States, could actually use large quantities of whatever the underdeveloped countries could place on the world market. With no tradition of "colonialism" in the turbulent continents to the south, the Kremlin could make its pretense of "disinterestedness" appear exceedingly plausible.

With nothing to lose in the revolutionary efforts of Asia and Africa to dispossess the West, the Soviets encouraged the new nations in their neutralism. Anushan Agafonovich, Director of the Soviet Institute of World Economic and International Relations, assured the delegates to the Afro-Asian conference at Cairo in December, 1957, that Russian aid carried no military or political obligations. "We do not ask you," he said, "to participate in any blocs, reshuffle your governments or change your domestic or foreign policy. We are ready to help you as brother helps brother. . . . Tell us what you need and we will help you and send, according to our economic capabilities, money needed in the form of loans or aid . . . to build for you institutions for industry, education and hospitals. . . ."

Soviet ambitions expanded the cold war into the non-European world. Even the realization that too much violence anywhere might terminate in the destruction of the Russian homeland did not prevent the Kremlin from striving for every situation which promised some change in the status quo to the Soviet advantage. Outside Europe, then, coexistence meant conflict. It was synonymous with cold war. Here successful negotiations required nothing less than some previously established condition of stability capable of curtailing Soviet expectations. Until this existed, Western interests lay in resistance—in the continuance of the cold war.

The American Commitment to Stability. American purpose at mid-century stood in sharp contrast to that of the U.S.S.R. Whereas the Kremlin sought to maintain the status quo within its own sphere and encourage change in Africa and Asia, American policy was designed to create maximum change behind the Iron Curtain and to prevent it elsewhere. On both counts, this nation placed itself in opposition to the fundamental political and military realities of the age. This explains with some precision the perennial frustration of American ambitions throughout the Eastern Hemisphere.

That this nation should have revealed so little comprehension and appreciation of Afro-Asian nationalism was astonishing, for the anti-colonial upheaval owed its philosophical genesis more to Woodrow Wilson than to Lenin. It was little but the twentieth-century version of this nation's struggle for freedom and equality. The Declaration of Independence served to rationalize both revolutionary movements. But the United States in the twentieth century was no longer the tiny Republic which had identified its search for security and recognition with the progress of liberal revolution. By 1900 the American people discovered that they had achieved the best of all possible worlds. Thereafter they opposed any fundamental alterations in the worldwide political and economic structure as it had evolved under the aegis of the Western powers. To perpetuate that structure, the United States had entered the two world wars of this century. This nation's growing commitment to law and order came as well from its own democratic past which permitted it, with one notable exception, to resolve its great internal challenges with a minimum of disorder. The violence and hysteria of Afro-Asian nationalism after 1950 was strangely disturbing to a satisfied and complacent people, especially when that pressure for change tended to undermine the stability of a Western-dominated world which had served this nation so well. The logic which conceded all advantage in a turbulent and revolutionary world to the U.S.S.R. was simply the final motivation in dictating a status quo policy for the United States.

Perhaps the precise response of official Washington to the Afro-Asian upheaval was conditioned by events in China. Those who attributed the collapse of Chiang Kai-shek's regime to some combination of American subversion and Soviet aggression were forced to deny the very existence of nationalism as the determining force behind change in that country. This placed them and the nation in crucial dilemma. For how could they ignore the indigenous nature of revolution in China and still recognize its role in the general upheaval of Asia and Africa? Certainly no one attributed to the United States Department of State the independence of India, Ceylon, Burma, Pakistan, or Indonesia, or the civil war in Indochina. But with an iron logic, the American posture toward China forced American leadership, from fear or from conviction, to disregard in most of its fundamental decisions the tides of Afro-Asian nationalism. The nation's policy toward China corrupted beyond measure its attitudes toward change.

Chiang Kai-shek's retreat before the Communist-led revolutionary forces of China persuaded many Americans that Soviet communism was a special threat to Asia and Africa. What made the danger of expanding Communist penetration into the underdeveloped continents appear so acute was the theory that Marxism was antithetical to national sovereignty, and that communism would gradually destroy all national entities in Asia and create one vast community under Communist domination. To some American officials Chinese imperialism was merely the Asiatic agent for the new universalism. "The Soviet leaders, in mapping their strategy for world conquest," Secretary of State John Foster Dulles warned in November, 1953, "hit on nationalism as a device for absorbing the colonial peoples." The danger, continued his argument, rested in the ability of Communist agitators to aggravate the nationalist aspirations of people so that they would rebel violently against the existing order. Before a new stability could be created, the Communists would gain control of the nation and convey it into the Soviet orbit. So pronounced became this interpretation of pressures against the status quo in Asia that American policy tended to credit communism, emanating from Peiping and Moscow, rather than nationalism with stimulating revolutionary action against governments friendly to the West.

This analysis of change in Asia and Africa undoubtedly described Communist tactics and Communist intent with some accuracy. The conceptual problem which it created lay in its emphasis. No one would deny the disruptive role of Communist agents and guerrillas, or even of Soviet and Chinese officials, in any turbulent, jungle environment. But to assign the deep stirrings of the Afro-Asian world primarily to such factors eliminated from American thought much serious concern for the force of nationalism itself. Again, as did official American attitudes toward China, it tended to deny both the legitimacy and the historic significance of the entire revolutionary upheaval of the century. In failing to separate the independent cause of nationalism from its Communist detractors, the nation's spokesmen, in their single-minded opposition to change, overlooked the fundamental and unalterable importance of governmental efficiency and responsiveness in resisting Communist encroachment and viewed nationalism, which would of necessity find its expression in some organized leadership, as only an unfortunate emotion which exposed the subcontinents to perennial Communist exploitation.

Wherever in Asia Communist regimes triumphed or

threatened to do so, their leaders spoke the language of nationalism. Yet official Washington, in its concern over Communist expansion, often denied the essential role of nationalism in any genuine Communist success. Walter Robertson, Assistant Secretary of State for Far Eastern Affairs, for example, declared in a speech at Hampden-Sydney College in June, 1958, that communism, instead of riding the crest of nationalism, actually warred against it and, if successful, would bring the entire continent of Asia under the control of Peiping and Moscow. So completely did such argument anchor American interest to the status quo that one well known Indian leader declared that if his nation had not achieved its independence as early as 1947 the United States would have opposed it.

At times the American addiction for the status quo forced it to deny its own principle of self-determination of peoples. This doctrine asserts that every society has the right to establish its own objectives and to decide for itself which method is appropriate. It grants the right of revolution, and the right of revolution assumes the right to employ force. Speaking for another age, Thomas Jefferson advised that "a little rebellion, now and then, is a good thing, and as necessary in the political world as storms in the physical." Again he wrote: "The tree of liberty must be refreshed from time to time with the blood of patriots and tyrants." Whereas the Western world of the twentieth century abhorred the resort to political violence, it could suggest no alternative course of action for disposing of non-democratic governments.

To limit change in the contemporary world, the United States adopted the concept that change, to be legitimate, must be peaceful. President Dwight D. Eisenhower declared before the U.N. General Assembly in August, 1958, that the status quo was not sacrosanct and that change was the law of life and progress. "But when change reflects the will of the people," he added, "then change can and should be brought about in peaceful ways." How political change in much of the Afro-Asian world could be achieved peacefully was not made clear. This strange doctrine that change was legitimate only if peaceful was illustrated by the cartoon depicting an emaciated Arab tribesman held to the desert sand by a well-fed sheik. At the side stood Mr. Dulles, shaking his finger in the face of the prostrate tribesman and informing him that it was permissible to revolt provided that he did so peacefully. Such dogma insisted that other peoples and societies really had no right to make essential decisions for themselves. And to the extent that the United States employed its resources to prevent change in other nations, it defied its own fundamental principle of self-determination. V. K. Krishna Menon, after challenging the American concept of legitimacy before the U.N. General Assembly in 1960, invited the United States delegation to read the Declaration of Independence. "Legitimism," he declared, "cannot be defended, and if you object to revolutionary governments, then you simply argue against the whole of progress."

United States Alliances in Asia. That rationale which attributed change to Communist aggression rather than indigenous nationalism gave the United States no intellectual choice but to place its emphasis on military alliances to prevent that change which it did not want. The Korean War tended to substantiate the validity of the military response in the Far East, for here indeed the threat to the status quo was one of military aggression. But the Korean War remained an isolated example. Elsewhere the pressures for change, whether Communist-led or not, responded to indigenous conditions.

Indochina demonstrated that revolutionary change could not be prevented by military means. The Indochinese civil war, raging since 1946, went steadily against the French. Observers on the scene understood clearly that the strength of the revolutionary forces of Ho Chi Minh sprang from the nationalistic fervor of the countryside, implemented by rebel promises and the fear of reprisal as well as the general desire of the masses to rid the country of French rule. But to Washington officials the fact that Ho was an avowed Communist reduced the civil war, aimed primarily at national independence and so regarded by the countries of Asia, to a Communist aggression emanating from Peiping. The final crisis came with the siege of Dienbienphu in the spring of 1954. Having warned repeatedly that the French province was the key to all Southeast Asia, Secretary Dulles had no alternative but to revise downward the American estimation of the region's strategic importance or to commit the United States to a unilateral defense of the province. Early in January, 1954, he had announced to the world his new policy of "massive retaliation." (*See Document No. 9.*) Now he threatened to apply it to Indochina. This retreat to a purely military policy denied at a critical moment both the existence and the legitimacy of Indochinese nationalism as a challenge to French colonial rule. Many Americans lauded the new doctrine as an inexpensive device to prevent unwanted change in Asia. The Chinese Reds called the bluff and proceeded to support the Indochinese insurgents. Dienbienphu fell in the late spring of 1954. Because external aggression was not the central issue, there was nothing that the United States could do to save the French position. There was no military defense against violent ideas, especially when those ideas had a legitimacy demonstrated by the entire history of the modern world. (*See Document No. 10.*)

To strengthen the regimes along the Chinese periphery against pressure from Peiping and Moscow, now regarded by Washington officials as the primary and at times the only cause of Asian instability, the United States constructed its Asian policy around a series of alliances aimed at the containment of communism. These pacts included, in addition to the earlier treaties with Japan, the Philippines, Australia, and New Zealand, a mutual defense agreement with the Republic of Korea, in October, 1953, and the Southeast Asia Treaty Organization, negotiated in the fall of 1954. SEATO, the basic treaty structure in Asia, comprised the United States, England, France, Australia, New Zealand, Pakistan, Thailand, and the Philippines. These eight nations agreed to act jointly against "any fact or situation which might endanger the peace of the "area" south of Formosa. As a military arrangement it was of doubtful value, for the only nations that could have made it a success in building the needed balance of power in the Orient to offset the expanding strength of China—India, Burma, Ceylon, and Indonesia—refused to join it. These four nations preferred to maintain their neutralist position in the conflict that centered in the United States and mainland China.

For the United States, SEATO was aimed at stopping the spread of international communism through armed force. But because such a threat of open aggression was remote and common action almost impossible, the pact required little of its Asian members but a verbal commitment to anti-communism. On the other hand, the Asian signatories could make special claims on the United States for financial and political support. Whatever compatibility of interest flowed from the American desire for allies and the Asian desire for American aid, it did not cover the specific and crucial question of the future of China. For its inconsequential military support the United States was willing to pay a high political price. By furnishing arms to Pakistan, for example, it placed an enormous military and financial burden on India, a nation of even greater concern to the United States.

In December, 1954, Secretary Dulles completed the American alliance system in Asia by negotiating a mutual defense treaty with the Republic of China on Formosa. The agreement with Chiang Kai-shek prevented any Nationalist Chinese forays against the mainland by establishing the requirement that all use of force in the Formosan Straits be a matter of joint agreement unless the question were self-defense. Japanese internal development throughout the fifties, plus the conviction that the nuclear stalemate made an alliance with the United States increasingly dangerous, prompted the Japanese government to demand greater voice in the alliance. In the new treaty of January, 1960, the United States again secured the use of Japanese facilities and areas for its military forces. But the Japanese reserved the right to determine how American troops on Japanese soil would be deployed, for the Japanese were determined not to be drawn into a war, especially against mainland China, by the support which the United States would require of its Japanese bases.

For the active defense of Southeast Asia the United States carried a unilateral burden, for budgetary considerations limited the defense of the region to massive retaliation. To create a military establishment for Asia, Mr. Dulles admitted before Congress, would be "an injudicious overextension of our military power. We do not have the adequate forces to do it," he explained, "and I believe that if there should be an open armed attack in that area the most effective step would be to strike at the source of the aggression rather than to try to rush American manpower into the area to try to fight a ground war."

What value the alliance system would have in repelling attack was not clear, for the Asian nations possessed only conventional weapons and Mr. Dulles warned that this nation would not support another local war. By his admission there were no ground forces within the alliance structure that would be effective against the armies of mainland China. In the event of aggression, therefore, the forces in Southeast Asia could serve only as a trip wire to bring the nuclear weapons of the United States into play. Such a defense system required no alliances at all. If this nation's interests were actually challenged by Chinese aggression, moreover, American power would be brought to bear as readily in defense of Burma or India as for Thailand or Pakistan.

Alliances vs. Neutralism. Alliances became the measure of American success in building centers of resistance toward the Soviet bloc. This perennial search for allies was predicated on the assumption of a divided world in which no nation would choose neutrality. Mr. Dulles, referring to the agreements which had built the American alliance system, made this clear at Iowa State University in June, 1956: "These treaties abolish, as between the parties, the principle of neutrality, which pretends that a nation can best gain safety for itself by being indifferent to the fate of others. This has increasingly become an obsolete conception and, except under very exceptional circumstances, it is an immoral and shortsighted conception. The free world today is stronger, and peace is more secure, because so many free nations courageously recognize the now demonstrated fact that their own peace and safety would be endangered by assault on freedom elsewhere." That freedom of choice on which this nation relied as recently as 1941 was now denied to others as immoral behavior.

But this purpose of bipolarizing the world soon demonstrated its limitations. Most nations rejected the concept of a divided world. They refused to enter any military arrangement with the West at all, for they regarded the postwar structure of world politics as neither stable nor permanent. The very notion of a world divided into two all-encompassing spheres, in which nations could be accurately categorized as friends or enemies, was unrealistic, for national interests were too varied and fluid. Indeed, in every Asian crisis of the fifties, this nation's allies, both European and Asian, behaved as neutrals. This reluctance of most nations to identify themselves with the United States in world affairs, especially in time of crisis, gradually forced American officials to adopt an ambivalent view toward neutralism. Frederick W. Jandrey, Deputy Assistant Secretary of State for European Affairs, expressed the newer American attitude with some precision in May, 1958:

> We fully respect the right of any state to choose neutrality. We would never try to compel a nation to join a collective security system against its will. But this does not mean that we are obliged to agree with its reasoning. It would have been comparatively easy for the United States itself to have retreated to a policy of neutrality and isolation after World War II. . . . Fortunately . . . we took a more far-sighted view. . . . But just as we ourselves have recognized our inability to "go it alone," so do we believe that, in the long run, *no* free nation can successfully go it alone. . . . The Soviet Union and its Communist handymen have never respected either neutrality or nationality. To them, a neutral is simply a potential victim.

For many statesmen and students of world affairs the powerful trend toward neutralism comprised the world's best hope of avoiding World War III. It promised after 1950 to replace the immediate postwar movement toward bipolarism with a countering movement toward an older and more normal multiplicity and flexibility in world politics, and to permit nations outside the power blocs to blunt the sharp edges of the East-West military conflict. Indeed, in every major crisis of the fifties—Korea, Indochina, and Formosa—it was neutralist pressure as much as any other factor that kept the struggle limited.

A nation's security is determined less by its formal alliances than by the sheer quality of its foreign policies. Merely furnishing military equipment to allies requires neither imagination nor specific knowledge of competing national interests. No nation concedes its right of decision to another simply through the act of signing a document. Its allegiance to any understanding can be won only through the constant wisdom of policy, for in any conflict it has but one obligation—to seek out its own interests. It is mutual interest, not formal alliance, that determines whether nations will stand together in a crisis. If this nation's allies failed to support it in any controversy vis-à-vis the Chinese mainland. it was because their attitudes toward Peiping's position in Asiatic affairs did not coincide with those of the United States. The challenge of change demanded policies anchored less to ephemeral agreements, however formal and impressive, than understanding and tolerance.

Unfortunately the indiscriminate search for receptive, pro-Western factions in Asia and Africa prompted United States officials at times to support narrow-based and irresponsible governments, incapable of stimulating the patriotic devotion of their peoples. Poorly-governed states could hardly be useful as allies, especially when the arms they received were employed largely to sustain their avowedly anti-Communist regimes from their internal enemies. "As a consequence of our concentration on military pacts and doctrines," Senator J. William Fulbright observed in July, 1958, "there are few of the newly independent countries in the world in which we have an understanding of the motivations of the common man. In most countries, the United States has dealt with princes, potentates, big business, and the entrenched, frequently corrupt, representatives of the past." Yet in official American policy there was no recognition of legitimacy in revolutionary pressures against even such regimes.

To achieve domestic stability, new nations required both the opportunity for genuine self-determination and sufficient economic expansion to assure some progress toward the satisfaction of domestic requirements. Sukarno denied that military aid contributed anything to Western security, either in building effective military establishments or in assuring responsible governments. Nations receiving military equipment, he warned Congress in 1956, merely became more dependent on the United States and less worthwhile as partners. It was essential for Asian security, he said, that the countries of that continent disposed of their domestic challenges with some efficiency, for the greater their internal achievements and sense of national pride, the greater would be their determination to defend themselves against external enemies.

The Eisenhower Doctrine. This established habit of evaluating all revolutionary tendencies in the Afro-Asian world in purely cold war terms forced the nation's leadership to ignore the myriad of non-Communist forces at work in every crisis of the fifties. Behind every political upheaval of the decade was the desire for a higher stage of governmental efficiency and responsiveness to the needs of long-oppressed peoples for a better life and a greater measure of self-realization. In every revolution or riot there was the search for the substance as well as the promise of a more democratic order. Throughout Asia dissident elements requested of their governments more determined efforts to avoid big-power alignments. But official Washington, in its continuing effort to resist change, attributed the growing instability of many American-backed governments to communism rather than the demand for greater national self-determination in both domestic and international affairs. This stereotyped American response was clear in every major upheaval of the late fifties. It lay at the heart of the famed Eisenhower Doctrine.

Middle Eastern instability, following the Suez crisis of November, 1956, required some declaration of United States policy. To meet the new responsibilities occasioned by the momentary deflation of traditional British and French influence in the region, President Eisenhower, on January 5, 1957, requested that Congress sponsor a joint resolution which would offer economic aid to the Middle Eastern nations "desiring such assistance in the development of economic strength dedicated to the maintenance of national independence." To guarantee the integrity of such nations, the resolution added that "if the President determines the necessity thereof, the United States is prepared to use armed forces to assist any such nation or group of such nations requesting assistance against armed aggression from any country controlled by international communism." Middle Eastern instability, the President charged, had been heightened by Soviet efforts to dominate the region. The resolution recognized no challenge to the status quo in the Middle East except that of Communist aggression or subversion. It designated the Middle East specifically as a battleground of the cold war. Denying the strength of neutralism in the Middle East, Vice President Nixon observed that the outcome of the crisis in the Arab world would be determined "by what happens to the millions of people who are trying to decide whether they will align themselves with the Communist nations or with the free nations."

Critics everywhere agreed that the Eisenhower Doctrine contained two basic fallacies. First, it obscured the legitimate role of nationalism in Middle Eastern instability. Moreover, it was Israel, Britain, and France, not international communism, that had threatened the status quo in the Suez crisis. Second, the Eisenhower Doctrine committed the United States to the status quo in a region where there were few if any viable political entities. Some of the Middle Eastern states, such as Lebanon and Jordan, were hardly "nations" at all. Conditions were ripe for revolt in Iraq, Lebanon, and Jordan. In Iraq revolution had been smoldering for a decade. When Nuri-es-Said, its pro-Western premier, dissolved the Parliament in 1954, in which the opposition was less than thirty out of 144, his opponents were convinced that change would require a revolution. In Lebanon, President Camille Chamoun enjoyed only limited popularity after the elections of 1957. His oppositions did not necessarily represent "anti-Western" elements, but in significant degree simply the "outs." The Jordanian government was renowned for its nepotism and corruption. So unstable was his throne that King Hussein was forced to entrust his life to White Russian bodyguards. Increasing this deep-seated instability within a number of pro-Western governments was Colonel Gamal Abdul Nasser's Pan-Arab movement, centering in Cairo, which warred on the governments of the individual Arab states in the interest of creating a greater Arab unity.

Within weeks of the announcement of the Eisenhower Doctrine the United States was called upon to defend that status quo. In April, 1957, a coup threatened to overthrow King Hussein. Syria, Egypt, Iraq, and Israel stood ready to intervene and, if necessary, partition the country. The President, acting under the new doctrine, despatched the Sixth Fleet to the Eastern Mediterranean. This demonstration of force, plus a huge grant of $10 million, bolstered the regime and gave it some stability. Several months later pro-Nasser forces in the Syrian army took control of that country. This new elite rejected American interference and in February, 1958, linked Syria to Egypt to form the United Arab Republic. In July, pro-Nasser elements in Iraq unleashed a revolt which terminated in the murder of King Faisal and Premier Nuri-es-Said and in the seizure of the Iraqi government. Convinced that the new regime was not pro-Communist, the United States quickly recognized it.

Strengthened by this successful coup, the Pan-Arab movement threatened to overturn the governments of Lebanon and Jordan. Both states appealed to the United States. An American army brigade, flown into Lebanon from West Germany, and a regiment of British paratroopers, dropped into Jordan, saved the two pro-Western governments. But this commitment to maintain all Middle Eastern regimes in power, whatever their quality or popularity, threatened the United States with permanent involvement in Middle Eastern affairs. There was no guarantee that many governments of the region could survive the withdrawal of foreign military support. Indeed, in 1960 the pro-Western Menderes government of Turkey, under serious indictment for repression, waste, corruption, and even atrocities, fell before a military junta. Pan-Arabism, with its appeal to the grandeur of Arab history, remained a powerful force, especially among Arab intellectuals. The boundaries which it sought to erase were largely artificial and meaningless. American officials seldom explained how Pan-Arabism threatened Western interests in the Middle East, but they knew that it endangered the status quo. This fact suggested why, under the Eisenhower Doctrine, the movement was not only opposed but also identified with Soviet expansion.

The Persistence of Revolution.   By 1960 one American-backed regime in Asia after another began to falter under the internal pressures for greater self-realization.

The political and moral price exacted from the perennial denial of self-determination, in the interest of sustaining purely anti-Communist regimes, was demonstrated clearly in a succession of revolts and riots in pro-Western countries.

Throughout the postwar period President Syngman Rhee of South Korea was second only to Chiang Kai-shek as the favorite of American diplomacy in the Far East. The United States had fought the Korean War in large measure to save him and his regime. His Liberal Party, supported by a police force of 300,000, enjoyed a monopoly in South Korean politics. After controlling a series of elections, Rhee attempted in March, 1960, to hand-pick his potential successor by maneuvering the victory of his long-time intimate, Lee Ki Poong, as Vice President. This initiated a wave of student protest which culminated on April 19 in a mass uprising of more than 100,000 persons in Seoul, the Korean capital. In the rioting 140 people were killed. Rhee summoned his American-trained army to rescue his regime, but it refused to fire on the student-led mob. Rhee attempted simultaneously to bring the United States government to his support by instructing the Korean ambassador in Washington, You Chan Yang, to announce that the riots were Communist-inspired. Learning that he had been purposely misinformed, Yang submitted his resignation.

Eventually under American pressure, Rhee agreed to go into semi-retirement and secure the resignation of Lee. But on April 25 another riot forced his total capitulation. That his government had never been democratic was known to American officials, but stability seemed a better defense than democracy against the Communist enemy. President Eisenhower, at his news conference of April 27, simply deplored the resort to violence in Korea.

With the failure of massive retaliation to save Indochina for the French in 1954, the United States government determined to build up the neighboring kingdom of Laos into "a bulwark against Communism." During the next five years that country received more aid on the basis of its three million population than any other country in the world. Those funds were used to support an anti-Communist regime, admittedly undemocratic, whose only obligation to this nation was to use its army to fight the Communist Pathet Lao forces of northern Laos. The election which brought the right-wing government into power was blatantly rigged. It denied both the Communist and neutralist elements of the country a single electoral seat. The perennial failure of the Laotian government to stabilize the country was evidence of its inability to create any popular support among the village populations.

When this regime was overthrown by a military coup engineered by Captain Kong Le, a rebel leader, in August, 1960, the Asian press termed the uprising another failure of American policy in the Far East. The Bangkok *World* pointed to the anti-Americanism of the new regime as "another aspect of . . . the dilemma of funneling aid through unpopular and possibly corrupt governments." Le accused the deposed leadership of warring on Pathet Lao merely to obtain money from the United States, for obviously the war had been conducted with little enthusiasm. The new premier, Prince Souvanna Phouma, promised to call off the civil war and make Laos a neutral in the cold war. But he failed in this purpose. The right wing, under pro-American Phoumi Nosavan who controlled the army, overthrew the neutralist government and continued to fight the Communist guerrillas. By the end of 1960 the Soviet Union had begun to support the Pathet Lao forces openly with military equipment, threatening to bring another Indochina-type struggle to that land-locked country.

Again in Japan the United States was victimized in 1960 by its refusal to recognize any opposition, except communism itself, to its purpose of building one vast anti-Communist bloc in the Far East. The Kremlin warning, following the U-2 incident of May, that Russia would retaliate against any base used to launch further spy flights across Soviet territory, ignited a violent neutralist reaction among Japanese students especially. Such deep-seated convictions reflected, in part, the uniqueness of the Japanese experience. Many citizens of Japan had no intention of forgetting the atomic destruction of Hiroshima or the long American occupation; they had no interest in another war. They resented the defiance of the spirit of the Japanese constitution in the rebuilding of the Japanese military establishment. They observed that many Japanese officials, including Premier Nobusuke Kishi himself, had been part of the old order. Long before the U-2 flights Japanese neutralists had challenged their government's military arrangement with the United States.

This growing opposition to Japanese military policy culminated in bitter attacks on the renewal of the mutual defense pact. Premier Kishi rammed the new treaty through the lower house of the Diet late on the night of May 20 after the Socialist opposition had been removed bodily from the chamber for creating a disturbance. Under the Japanese constitution the treaty would be ratified automatically in thirty days whether approved by the upper house or not, provided the Diet was not dissolved in the meantime. Much of the rioting of May and June was designed to force the resignation of the Kishi government.

Eventually the Japanese demonstrations were directed at President Eisenhower's scheduled visit of early June, for Kishi's opponents interpreted the visit as an effort to bolster his regime and save the treaty. When the President reached Manila on his Far Eastern tour, 20,000 rioters stormed the Japanese Diet in the most violent demonstration yet staged against the treaty, the Kishi regime, and the President's visit. During a wild night of rioting one person was killed and almost a thousand, including 600 police, were injured. Kishi met with his cabinet and announced to reporters that he would ask the President to cancel his visit. In Manila Mr. Eisenhower accepted the decision of the Japanese government with sympathetic understanding. The Kishi government withstood the siege until the treaty went into effect and then resigned.

In his report to the nation late in June, the President said: "It seems apparent that the Communists some time ago reached the conclusion that these visits were of such positive value to the Free World as to obstruct Communist imperialism. . . . With their associates in Peiping, they went to great lengths and expense to create disorders in Tokyo that compelled the Japanese government to decide . . . that it should revoke its long-standing invitation for me to visit that sister of democracy." Undoubtedly Japanese Communists were out in force during the riots. But the President's report not only absolved United States policy of all responsibility for the Tokyo demonstrations, but also refused to acknowledge the existence, much less the legitimacy, of neutralism as a factor in Japanese thought.

The Problem of Self-Determination in a Divided World. For the new nations of Asia and Africa the great problem of the fifties was that of preserving their struggle against the past without becoming involved in the great contest of power between the U.S.S.R. and the West. Why this proved to be difficult was obvious. In every revolutionary situation extremists of right or left, with little interest in popular government, were willing to seek the moral and physical support of the outside world with their stereotyped appeals to communism or anti-communism. Because the big powers, always in search of some ideological advantage, were usually ready to intervene, every major upheaval of the fifties tended eventually to expose the conflict of interest between the United States and the U.S.S.R. Self-determination was generally the loser. It was not strange, therefore, that the authentic and established leaders of Asia and Africa bitterly opposed those who managed, through their rhetoric even more than their actions, to excite the anxieties of the great cold war rivals.

American efforts to preserve the status quo outside Europe overreached the nation's resources and interests as much as did its goal of liberation inside the Soviet sphere. Through a wide variety of involvements the United States committed itself to a state of siege along the entire southern periphery of the Soviet bloc under the conviction that the actions of Peiping and Moscow prevented the peaceful evolution of the Afro-Asian world. Actually not one revolution in Asia or Africa throughout the postwar period presented a simple struggle between freedom and tyranny. Yet the United States, from its underestimation of the world's revolutionary fervor, continued to define the cold war in both moral and global terms and to deny officially that the Afro-Asian nations had interests and ambitions quite separate from those of the United States and the Soviet Union—that the world was, in fact, divided into three parts.

It was ironic that this nation generally ignored the principle of self-determination in Asia and Africa where it had some chance of success and promoted it behind the Iron and Bamboo curtains where it had no chance of success at all. But too often Americans behaved as if communism were the host rather than the parasite of change. Adlai Stevenson challenged this tendency when he declared, "The beginning of wisdom in the West, I think, is to have our own creative policy—not just a negative policy to stop the Communists, but one that reflects our own vision of a viable world society and our own understanding of the revolutions through which we live." Only when the United States recognized officially that past changes, whatever their magnitude, were not synonymous with Communist aggression would it discard its feeling of universal obligation, eliminate the nagging character of its diplomacy, and cease to respond to every episode as if it were ushering in the Day of Judgment.

— 6 —

ENDS WITHOUT MEANS

Fifteen years had passed by 1960 since Soviet repression in Eastern Europe first destroyed the promise of great power unity in the postwar world. Despite the continued enormity of the resulting cold war, the United States as a nation was more divided than ever before on the meaning of the Russian challenge. In a sense this confusion was understandable, for there were elements in the conflict that had no clear precedent in history—the sheer destructiveness of modern weapons, the huge military establishments, and the multiple nature and persistence of international pressures. But increasingly the East-West conflict widened the dichotomy between two American concepts of the Soviet threat: first, that the struggle continued to be circumscribed by traditions of power politics and national interest, and, second, that it had evolved into a limitless contest between freedom and tyranny on a global scale, a totally revolutionary phenomenon propelling history down its final, dangerous course. American reactions to the cold war varied from absolute dread that nuclear destruction might terminate civilization itself to the utter impatience that the West continued to tolerate the existence of the Communist system at all.

Policies required to span such a chasm of thought and concept could only be indecisive, confused, and inconsistent. Eventually any nation, if it would conduct itself responsibly in world affairs, must determine with some precision the peril which it faces. The persistent overestimation of danger provokes the nation to demand too much of itself and of the enemy simply to guarantee that enough will be demanded; the persistent underestimation of danger undermines its determination to protect even what is essential. The first tendency produces within the adversary the emotion of fear; the second, of overconfidence. Either reaction contains within itself the seeds of aggression and war. Any rational and consistent response to the Russian challenge required, therefore, some reasonably accurate evaluation not only of Soviet intention but also of Soviet power available to achieve it.

There was much in the United States-Soviet conflict that flowed logically from the past. Such extended struggles have been common enough in history, for great nations have usually found themselves in competition for prestige and security, sea lanes and resources, markets and even empires. That such a rivalry would eventually embrace the United States and Russia had been predicted for over a century. In the eighteen-thirties Alexis de Tocqueville, the brilliant French critic of American democracy, pointed to the two nations as the great powers of the future, and observed that "each of these seems to be marked out by the will of heaven to sway the destinies of half the globe." In the next decade Alexander Herzen, the Russian liberal, denied that human destiny was nailed to Western Europe. He saw in the United States and Russia two young, vigorous nations which were preparing themselves to wield the power that once belonged to Europe. It seemed inescapable that these two aspiring giants, with their extensive territories, temperate climates, energetic populations,

and abundant resources, would come to the forefront of
world politics as major contestants for prestige and power.
In a sense the cold war had been a traditional struggle,
conducted in an historic context, the mere fulfillment of
prophecy.

The Concept of Global Conspiracy. Throughout the
decade of the fifties this limited concept of the cold war
received scant attention in the United States. Most American officials, political leaders, and writers accepted the
notion that the Soviet Union represented a global conspiracy. They argued that the Kremlin was concerned
less with stabilizing its postwar position than with dominating the free world. What mattered fundamentally to
them was the irreconcilable conflict between freedom and
an ideology that aimed at the complete subjugation of the
individual through the rule of terror. They regarded Soviet
communism as a virus that could not be contained; if permitted to exist, it would destroy freedom everywhere. The
Communist movement, Charles Malik of Lebanon, former
president of the U.N. General Assembly, warned in 1960,
sought "to overthrow every existing government, regime,
system, outlook, religion and philosophy and bring the
whole world—all human thought, aspiration, action and
organization—under its absolute control." For some
American writers the cold war was merely the continua-
tion of a vast ideological assault on the free world that
began with the Bolshevik triumph of 1917 and had been
perpetuated by the absolute faith of Lenin, Stalin, and
Khrushchev in the ultimate victory of the Communist
system.

In this context of total conflict Soviet maneuvering
could not be accepted as traditional Russian behavior but
only as an integrated scheme to divide and confuse the
free world, to throw it off balance, to promote its collapse.
There was much in Soviet action to substantiate such
conclusions. The Kremlin introduced uncertainty and
abused the normal privileges of diplomacy; it violated
flagrantly previous agreements and turned high-level conferences into political forums. Toward regions outside its
sphere the Soviet Union maintained a varied offensive
which combined military, political, economic, and psychological methods. It exploited violence to further its ends;

it kept the world under constant tension by maintaining its armed might, by blustering and threatening. Senator Barry Goldwater, in his book, *The Conscience of a Conservative*, summarized the Soviet challenge in such terms: "We are confronted by a revolutionary world movement that possesses not only the will to dominate absolutely every square mile of the globe, but increasingly the capacity to do so. . . ." The Senator pointed specifically to the Soviet military power which rivaled that of the United States, the superior propaganda skills of the Kremlin, and the Communist ideology which imbued its adherents with a sense of historical mission. These powerful resources, he added, were "controlled by a ruthless despotism that brooks no deviation from the revolutionary course."

Soviet leaders did little to dispel such fears. They announced repeatedly their purpose of world domination. Nikita Khrushchev's words especially were characterized by a disturbing arrogance. At a Kremlin reception in November, 1956, he stated the oft-quoted but not exceptional phrase, "Whether you like it or not, history is on our side. We will bury you." The Soviet leader used every occasion to stress the superiority of the Communist system. Capitalism will perish, he warned, just as feudalism perished earlier. "All the world will come to communism," he declared in June, 1957. "History does not ask whether you want it or not." The Soviet Premier warned the West that the underlying Soviet purpose transcended the policies and actions of the moment. "People say our smiles are not honest," he once observed. "That is not true. Our smile is real and not artificial. But if anyone believes that our smile means that we have given up the teachings of Marx, Engels, and Lenin, he is badly mistaken."

Khrushchev's new economic policies appeared at once more hopeful and more threatening. These policies, anchored to an expanding Soviet economy, were designed to bring Soviet action into conformity with Soviet purpose. They were, in the words of the Soviet Premier, a device for dominating the world without military conquest. The new Russian imperialism moved forward on three fronts. It offered the Soviet model to the underdeveloped world; it sought to spread Soviet influence through programs of trade and aid; and, lastly, it threatened to reduce the

United States to a second-rank power through the achievements of the Soviet economy itself. Soviet productive power was thus to become a massive political weapon which would elevate Russian prestige and power throughout the world.

Anticipating the eventual triumph of the Soviet system through industry and technology alone, the Kremlin leaders attempted to call off the cold war in Europe if not in Asia and Africa. Their insistence that the struggle between communism and capitalism henceforth be peaceful reflected a realistic judgment of the destructiveness of modern war. If this was a denial of Marxist dogma on the inevitability of war, it meant that Khrushchev, unlike Marx, had some knowledge of hydrogen bombs. The relaxation of tension had the dual advantage of permitting a greater concentration of productive energy and resources within Russia itself and of producing greater complacency in the Western world. The Soviet plea for "peaceful coexistence" did not promise any reduction of goals; it illustrated simply the Kremlin's burgeoning confidence in nonmilitary means in its continuing, if partially concealed, offensive against the non-Communist world.

The Goal of Total Victory. American leaders warned the nation repeatedly against the acceptance of a Soviet-inspired peace. Such an acceptance, Secretary of State Dulles declared in April, 1955, would lead to the degradation of the human race. The Secretary added: "The Communist leaders know that, if pacifism becomes a prevalent mood among the free peoples, the Communists can easily conquer the world. Then they can confront the free peoples with successive choices between peace and surrender; and if peace is the absolute good, then surrenders become inevitable." The Soviet challenge was so insidious and pervading that it simply permitted no relaxation or compromise. Similarly Andrew H. Berding, Assistant Secretary of State for Public Affairs, appraised Soviet intentions following the Khrushchev visit to the United States in September, 1959, in these words:

We have noted a partial change in Soviet tactics. The Soviets have seemed somewhat more amenable, less aggressive, more relaxed, less provocative. . . . But, while Soviet tactics seem to have changed, we have been able thus far to detect no change whatever in Soviet ultimate ambitions—the creation of a Communist world. . . . They know that in a major war the Soviet Union would suffer devastation many, many times greater than the terrible losses they experienced in the last war. Therefore the thesis of Lenin that war is necessary to overcome capitalism has evidently been modified. But the conflict will be waged just the same, and with the same intensity as if it were military. The battlefields will be political, economic, psychological. There is every reason to believe that the Soviets will employ all means possible to triumph in all these fields.

Traditionally peace was the absence of war. Unfortunately, by 1960 it was no longer that simple, for the concept of a global Soviet conspiracy dictated that peace, to be genuine, had to be total. If one assumed that the Soviet Union would never concede its goal of dominating the globe, then the cold war would continue until either freedom or communism was destroyed. Either Russia would be driven back, its victims liberated, or it would steadily and inevitably take over the free world. It was essential, therefore, that American policy pursue not coexistence, but ultimate victory. "Like it or not," Eugene Lyons wrote, "the great and inescapable task of our epoch is not to end the Cold War but to win it." Peace would be tolerable only when it followed a victory over communism. Meanwhile the West dared not accept the status quo behind the Iron Curtain because it represented a necessary triumph for international communism in its career of world conquest.

But by the standards of total victory successful policy demanded more. Some writers and politicians suggested that the United States seek no less than the liberalization of the Kremlin and the granting of freedom to the Soviet peoples, for only the destruction of one-man rule could guarantee the ultimate security of the West. To protect Asia from subversion and conquest, some demanded more hostile and aggressive policies toward Peiping for the purpose of eliminating that regime entirely. According to the doctrine of global conflict the nation really had little choice. The cold war, Secretary Berding declared, is a "constant battle for victory, of one over the other, ultimate total triumph, and ultimate total defeat."

Peace between the United States and the U.S.S.R., then, could not exist until all problems were solved and all men had been freed. Only when freedom and justice prevailed would Soviet power cease to threaten the world. Peace, declared President Dwight D. Eisenhower at Paris in December, 1957, is not "an uneasy absence of strife bought at the price of cowardly surrender of principles. We cannot have peace and ignore righteous aspirations and noble heritages. The peace we do seek is an expanding state of justice and understanding. It is a peace within which men and women can freely exercise their unalienable rights to life, liberty, and the pursuit of happiness." In his Christmas message of December, 1959, the President again made it clear that the United States did not regard mere coexistence as a satisfactory arrangement for mankind. "After all," he said, "an uneasy coexistence can be as barren and sterile, joyless and stale of life for human beings as the coexistence of cell-mates in a penetentiary or labor camp." The United States, he added, anticipated the day when all the world would be free and enjoy a peace in which all peoples could engage in an open exchange of goods and ideas and contribute fully to the progress and prosperity of the world.

By the late fifties the notion that the United States dare settle for nothing less than victory appeared capable of capturing the entire nation. One group of distinguished clergymen declared, quite characteristically, in national convention: "Without freedom under God for every man and for every nation there can be no peace." Similarly Vice President Richard M. Nixon observed during the 1960 campaign that "as long as any man or woman is not free any place in the world, freedom is threatened where it exists. . . ." David Sarnoff, conceiving of national purpose in terms of universal principles, added dramatically in a noted essay of 1960, "Our message to humankind must be that America has decided, irrevocably, to win the cold war." Any lesser purpose would merely consign the United States and its principles to oblivion.

Ends Without Means. What the postwar generation had witnessed in world politics was essentially the manifestations of an unprecedented power revolution. It was the effort of Russia and China to establish a new order in international affairs that placed such an enormous burden on American foreign policy. Successful diplomacy demands the constant evalution of changing power relationships among nations and the resulting shifts in national interest, for any revolution in the force which other nations can bring to bear on world politics must either prompt a general, if reluctant, concession to the new realities or actuate the creation of a countering force to undo the change. At heart the American dilemma in the cold war was the nation's inability to choose either alternative. For many national leaders the power revolution wrought by the rise of the Soviet Union was too threatening and too immoral to be accepted diplomatically. What remained was either inaction, supported by the rhetoric of disapprobation, or the establishment of policies designed to roll the Soviet Union back to its boundaries of 1939 and to recreate the power balance of the thirties. Unfortunately the many Americans who clung to the exceedingly ambitious ends of total victory neglected almost entirely the question of means.

This nation's basic response to the Soviet challenge was military. At one time it was assumed that the West, with its capacity to outperform the U.S.S.R. in industrial production, could, through successful containment, give the inconsistencies within Russia time to undermine the entire Soviet structure. The experience of a decade of almost exclusive attention to nuclear armament demonstrated, however, that Western military preparedness would never be sufficient in itself to force any agreement on the Kremlin. The high hopes of American policy slowly disintegrated under the constant search for military strength which always seemed to elude the nation. The West did not win the race for military power, and it was clear after the launching of Sputnik in 1957 that no conceivable Western military establishment could achieve any declared purpose of American policy without war. Perhaps the satellites could not be freed even through war, for the resulting destruction would leave little worth liberating. Western military strength, despite its unprecedented magnitude, was still limited. And it was the vast discrepancy between ends and means that produced both inaction and embarrassment in the recurring crises of the postwar years.

But the persistent failure of the nation to dismantle the Soviet empire did not reduce the ends of policy; it merely sent men in a frantic search for other, more effective, means to close the gap between the goal of total victory and the experience of limited power.

In general those who continued to search for the means that would assure the ultimate Western triumph over communism found them in various forms of psychological warfare. This strategy became the foundation of the policy of boldness that sought to bring liberation to those behind the Iron Curtain through the rhetoric of freedom disseminated largely through massive radio towers. Upholding such methods of psychological warfare, Representative O. K. Armstrong of Missouri declared in February, 1952: "Let us realize this great and fundamental truth: That the struggle against communism is the struggle for minds and hearts of mankind. It cannot be won by bombs and guns alone. The strongest weapon that we hold in our hands is truth itself." Such a policy of liberation would succeed, Senator Thomas J. Dodd of Connecticut wrote in the summer of 1959, because it was "in harmony with the moral principles on which our faith and civilization are based."

This tendency to concede almost limitless power to words conformed to the deep-seated habit of attributing everything dangerous in the postwar world to Soviet ideology, not Soviet power. It was international communism that was the root of all evil. It was this insidious movement that created the monolithic Soviet bloc which included Red China, that stimulated and guided the revolutionary currents of Asia and Africa, that built the industrial and scientific bases of Soviet achievement. Having started at zero four decades earlier, it had by mid-century gained control of one-third of the world's population and was still reaching outward. But to those who discovered in communism, not in the force unleashed by Soviet productivity and Afro-Asian nationalism, the fundamental threat to traditional Western security, the danger never represented more than a body of ideas. Countering policy, therefore, demanded largely competing thoughts and words, not competing economic and military strength. This explained why those who accepted

the notion of world revolution never placed any strain
on the national budget.

If words were the essential element of power, critics of
coexistence wondered why the West did not throw the
Soviets back on their heels by making the same boasts
that one day capitalism would conquer all Communist
values and drive them from the face of the earth. They
charged that those who denied the efficacy of such
methods were conceding the inevitability of Soviet domination. To them any preference for traditional methods of
diplomatic behavior, amid the progress of world revolution, merely illustrated the extent to which communism
had undermined the will of the free world.

Still another approach to the problem of total victory
was suggested by William S. Schlamm in his book, *Germany and the East-West Crisis: The Decisive Challenge to
American Policy* (1959). Rather than bargain with the
Soviets over the future of Germany, he wrote, the West
must grasp the offensive. In partnership with a heavily
armed West Germany, the United States, employing
threats of violence, must force the Russians out of East
Germany. This would succeed, he predicted, because the
Soviets had to avoid war. The West, having rolled the
Soviets out of one strategic position, would gain the momentum and soon drive the Russians behind their prewar
boundaries. Any Soviet resistance would indicate merely
that the Kremlin had changed its strategy and would have
attacked the West anyway. Such risks the West must
assume, he warned, for the mere desire to avoid conflict
would guarantee the eventual triumph of communism.
Senator Goldwater, proposing a similar course of action,
insisted that the United States support any future revolution behind the Iron Curtain with the threat of massive
retaliation if the Russians attempted to suppress it with
force. The Soviets would concede to Western demands,
he assured Americans, because they would not risk the
destruction of their whole system merely to prevent the
loss of one region.

Whatever the nature of Soviet global strategy, somehow
the postwar hegemony of the Kremlin in East-Central
Europe remained the key to the entire East-West conflict.
As Senator Dodd observed, "if the Soviet Union could

have the wisdom to withdraw to its prewar frontiers, tensions would disappear overnight and the whole world sleep better." What happened to the world revolution under such conditions was not clear. If the issue between the United States and the U.S.S.R. was world domination, as the Senator insisted, then how could the cold war be resolved merely by freeing Hungary and Poland? If the conflict centered in the misuse of Soviet power in Europe, then the global challenge was quite limited after all.

For Secretary Dulles the superiority of freedom over despotism alone assured the ultimate triumph of the West. To him the free world, given time, could win the cold war totally at no great cost to itself, for the Soviet weakness lay fundamentally in the human spirit. By combining its military, economic, and moral assets, the West could exploit that weakness. The time would come, Mr. Dulles declared in December, 1957, "when inevitably, the Soviet rulers will have to change their attitude toward their own people, toward the rest of the world." If the United States remained strong and at the same time made its own freedom and liberty a flaming example to the world, the people behind the Iron Curtain would feel it and sense it and demand more of it for themselves. That, he said, was the "strategy of victory." The Secretary voiced his conviction again in September, 1958, when he said, "If there is any one thing in the world that is inevitable, it is that human beings want for themselves a degree of personal freedom and liberty which is denied by communism. So I believe that it is inevitable sooner or later, that that desire for personal freedom will manifest itself. Therefore we do not accept the type of Communist rule that now prevails as a permanent situation anywhere in the world." It was this conviction that virtue would triumph over evil that encouraged Mr. Dulles to pursue goals that had no relationship to the power which he wielded.

The Fallacy of Total Conflict. Herein lay the fallacy in the concept of total threat and total response. Its adherents, from their morbid conviction that the West could not resist Soviet ideology or subversion, demanded the eventual destruction of the Communist system. Then they discovered the promise of ultimate victory over

Russian communism in the pervading weakness of the Communist system itself. This inconsistency explained the total lack of balance between ends and means in national action. For the ends of policy were predicated on the assumption that the adversaries were omnipotent, omniscient, monstrously efficient, unhampered by any problems of their own, in possession of frightening power, and bent only on the destruction of the free world. But the means of policy were based on the antithetical assumption that the Soviet system was a hollow shell, incapable of governing its own people, subject to destruction by weapons no more elaborate than words and radio transmitters. Either the Soviet Union was no threat at all, or such weapons for victory were totally inadequate.

This same absence of any serious balance between ends and means characterized the American posture toward China. With the accession of Mr. Eisenhower to the presidency, the nation's commitment to Chiang Kai-shek became one of unshakable determination. Such key leaders of the new administration as John Foster Dulles, Walter S. Robertson, and Arthur W. Radford perpetuated an attitude of uncompromising antagonism toward the mainland regime and created a rationale to justify it. (*See Document No. 11.*) They rushed into every Far Eastern crisis with strident appeals to the anti-Chinese sentiment which they had helped to create, but neither they nor the nation had any desire to pay the price of war to destroy the Chinese enemy. Nonrecognition expressed their faith that one day the Peiping regime would cease to exist. American action, Mr. Dulles explained, was based on the assumption that "international Communism's rule of strict conformity is, in China, as elsewhere, a passing and not a perpetual phase." It was the intention of the United States, he said, to speed that passing.

Those who anticipated the total elimination of Peiping through a firm posture of disapprobation were never troubled by doubt. If the Communist threat to Asia was so pervasive as to require Peiping's ultimate destruction, the American formula assured that result without war or diplomacy. The continued recognition and support of the Kuomintang on Formosa, a State Department memorandum assured the nation in August, 1958, "enables it to challenge the claim of the Chinese Communists to represent the Chinese people and keeps alive the hopes of those Chinese who are determined eventually to free their country of Communist rule." However powerful and threatening the enemy, its obliteration was always assured by the very ideological and moral aberrations which constituted the original danger itself. By such doctrine every challenge to the national will, once it had been designated repressive and thus a defiance of the human spirit, could not escape ultimate self-destruction. It was not clear how such expectations of victory, demanding no price at all, could serve as the basis of serious policy. (*See Document No. 12.*)

The assumption that the free world could triumph over the Communist enemy everywhere without war had no clear historic precedent. Certainly the weapons of co-existence, disturbing as they were, had less the power of conquest than did the weapons of war. Yet many Americans, admitting the limits of nuclear war, anticipated total victory through crusades of liberation alone. Such action could either remain meaningless or require more or less fighting, for it was doubtful if the Soviets would concede to a verbal assault what they would not even concede to a military threat. If it ever appeared that the United States might free the satellites, for example, through non-military techniques, war would be imminent indeed. For certainly the Soviets would not leave their weapons unused while they went down before a barrage of words. Peaceful liberation remained a possibility only as long as it demonstrated its utter futility.

The Limits of Soviet Power.   Obviously the Soviet offensive was varied and disturbing, but nowhere after 1945 did it reveal the overwhelming power attributed to its Communist structure. Communism failed as an exportable commodity; its success even in Russia was doubtful. The Soviet empire had been built, not through the revolutionary doctrines of Marx and Lenin, but through the power of the Red Army under Stalin. Not one square foot of territory was delivered to the Soviet Union through Communist revolution alone. Even in Czechoslovakia the massive weight of Soviet armies helped to demoralize the nation and aid the Communist coup of 1948. In none of the Soviet satellites did communism demonstrate any power to destroy national sentiment and tradition.

Direct Russian control extended only as far as the reach of the Red Army. Marshal J. B. Tito of Yugoslavia, the devoted Communist, defied Marxist internationalism so thoroughly that he withdrew his nation from the Soviet bloc. Hungary's Kadar-Münnich regime, established as a puppet by the Kremlin after the revolution of 1956, was subservient to Russian influence. During its first four years in power, however, it sought to bring internal unity to Hungary. The Hungarian people, tired of the cause of liberation after the United States' failure to support the revolution, resigned themselves to the new regime. But they were still Hungarian, and fifteen years of Soviet control did not diminish their patriotism. If the U.S.S.R. was unable to corrupt Hungary between 1945 and 1960, it was difficult to see how it could corrupt the entire world. Only through sheer force did the Soviets maintain their hegemony over East Germany, Poland, Hungary, and the other satellites.

Wladyslaw Gomulka of Poland was as dedicated to communism as were the Kremlin leaders. Yet he remained a true Polish patriot, concerned solely for the welfare of his country. Polish communism was cast in his image. Gomulka was often distressed at his nation's refusal to accept his doctrines, and his efforts to impose them as a national program often went beyond what the Kremlin believed expedient. If he carefully avoided differences with Moscow, it was because he feared that Soviet interference might destroy his program completely. Under Gomulka communism remained a Polish, not an international phenomenon.

Undoubtedly there was something exploitable for Russia in a revolutionary Afro-Asian world. If earlier in this century Western Europe alone maintained that vast colonial hegemony which blanketed much of Africa, the Middle East, and Asia, any nationalistic pressure against that status quo could only weaken Western power and influence. But the anti-Western revolutions themselves did not belong to Russia, and the Soviet triumphs were exceedingly limited. That very nationalism which contributed to revolution at once placed limits on the control which the

Soviets were permitted to exert. Western prestige and influence, moreover, did not necessarily decline with the
independence movements; in some countries, such as India, it actually increased. The Soviets gained nothing
militarily and little politically (China was a temporary
exception) from the vast change that swept the Orient
and Africa after 1945.

The reason was clear. Communism in Asia, as in Europe, remained subservient to nationalism. It gained the
ascendancy in China and Indo-China, and threatened to
do so elsewhere, but only by capturing control of some
aspect of an indigenous nationalistic movement. Even in
the Communist countries of Asia nationalism remained
the chief determinant, and no quantity of Soviet arms
would undermine its primacy unless they were accompanied by significant numbers of Russian troops. Mao
Tse-tung was devoted to Chinese, not Russian, interests.
That China, unlike Yugoslavia, remained in the Soviet
bloc revealed simply a current mutuality of interest. But
China, under the impact of its new nationalism, was more
determined to pursue its own destiny than ever before in
its history. For that reason, China in the twentieth century comprised a greater threat to the Soviet Union than
at any time after the days of the Mongols. The moment
could well come when the Soviets would rue the day that
Communists gained control of China. Should the Communist elites triumph elsewhere in Asia, their relationship
to the U.S.S.R. would be much the same—uneasy alliance
or Titoism. Indian Communists would still be Indians,
concerned with the future of India. Applying this type of
analysis to the Western world in general, Louis J. Halle
wrote: "A Communist United States might be no less
hostile to the Soviet Union than a liberal democratic
United States. Because its total resources could be more
easily mobilized, it might, in fact, be distinctly more
threatening." Subversion and revolution were not necessarily triumphant as methods of conquest in Asia because
successful Communist revolutionaries, riding the tide of
nationalism, were intense patriots, not traitors.

The Limits of Economic Imperialism.   It was even
less clear how the Soviet Union could dominate the world
with its new economic offensive. What mattered was capa-

bility, not intent. Soviet policies of trade and aid could elevate Russian prestige, create opportunities for strengthening the Soviet economy, build attitudes of friendship, and perhaps render some weak economies vulnerable to Soviet pressure. They could not do more. Throughout the previous four decades the foreign trade and investments of the United States were unprecedented. Whatever this vast economic activity brought to the United States, it did not include conquest or even much friendship. More often American economic preponderance was a source of resentment, and the more vulnerable it rendered other economies, the greater that resentment had been. No nation can annex another or even gain control of its external policies through trade and investment alone, any more than one nation can destroy the sovereignty of another through revolution. In either case the power of decision remains within the weaker nation.

Soviet industrial and technological achievement was a genuine threat to American prestige and greatness. But the concept that Soviet economic productivity alone could command the power to dominate much of the world was an exaggeration. First, few American economists accepted Mr. Khrushchev's prediction that communism would bury capitalism. They agreed that the Soviet economy had grown more rapidly than that of the United States; they admitted that this growth in itself gave a boost to Soviet prestige; but they did not agree that the Soviet economy could outstrip that of the United States in the long run. Henry Cabot Lodge, when United States Representative to the U.N., commented realistically on the challenge of the Soviet economy:

> I . . . do not dispute Chairman Khrushchev's right to challenge us. Nor am I worried by improving the lot of the Russian citizen. In fact I welcome it. But I do dispute the accuracy of his prophecy. If we do what we are capable of doing, the Soviet Union will never surpass us. A country which thrives on competition as we do—in business, in politics, in sport—should not shrink from the idea of competition. A nation which sees what tens of thousands of plans of independent producers can create in the way of new wealth need never worry about competition from a state which is run by a central bureaucracy.

Second, it was difficult to see any relationship between productive capacity and world domination. For fifty years American productivity faced no serious competitor abroad. That fact lowered the prestige of nations such as England and France; it even curtailed their industrial expansion and limited their prosperity. If it reduced them gradually to second-class powers, it did not destroy them. Nor did past decades of American economic supremacy destroy or even weaken the Soviet economy. It seemed illogical to assume that once Soviet production exceeded that of the United States, this nation would falter and collapse. To accept Soviet words as a clear prediction of history was to accept the strange doctrine that communism was superior even when it was behind. What mattered in the cold war, unfortunately, was the relationship between industrial capacity and national power. It was this that created a danger of incalculable proportions to the Western world. Were there no cold war between the United States and the Soviet Union, the question of the Russian economy would hardly have been an issue between them at all.

Third, if the United States chose to accept the Soviet boasts of conquest through productivity as serious, there was still no clear answer to the challenge in the realm of diplomacy. What kind of foreign policy could have guaranteed the curtailment of the Soviet economy? The United States had contributed comparatively little to its continued evolution. Any effort to destroy it through war would have sacrificed much of this nation's own remarkable economic structure. Soviet industrial expansion was a matter of historical change which had little connection with Mr. Khrushchev's words. If the U.S.S.R. had the necessary resources, energy, and efficiency to surpass the United States, this nation could no more stop the process than could a troubled Britain stop the onrush of the American productive system sixty years earlier. The new Soviet challenge could not be ignored, but the answer rested within the American industrial system itself.

Perhaps more troublesome to Western concepts of democratic progress in the world was the Soviet and Chinese example. For backward and crowded countries, lacking resources and capital funds, the United States could hardly serve as a model at all. This nation grew up in a spacious and richly-laden continent; its system and achievements could not be duplicated elsewhere. Walter Lippmann saw the dilemma clearly: "We cannot beat the Soviet example by our example. For we are not an example that backward peoples can follow, and unless we can manage to create an example which they *can* follow, we shall almost certainly lose the Cold War in Asia and Africa, and perhaps elsewhere."

Fortunately, national autonomy was still the key to the Afro-Asian world. If nations there chose communism, it was doubtful if the resulting economic structure would have any more similarity to Marxism than would an economic system based on liberal democracy resemble that of the United States. Whether they built on Western capital or on some modification of the Chinese system, they would remain African and Asian. Wherever they might secure their aid, they would grant no more than limited jurisdiction to any external power. As allies they would be liabilities; they would contribute little to their defense and demand miracles that no one could perform.

There remained the Marxist interpretation of history to which the Kremlin leaders paid verbal homage. Their persistence in intoning the Marxist incantations perpetuated tension and fear in a divided world. Westerners pointed to the nearly-fulfilled predictions of Adolf Hitler's *Mein Kampf,* forgetting that Hitler's success was based on military power which the West refused to counter, not on nonmilitary devices and ideology which supposedly gave meaning to the Soviet purpose of world domination. The Kremlin leaders were politicians. Unlike Hitler, they faced military force sufficient to prevent any drastic miscalculations. And their day-to-day decisions reflected a host of immediate problems, many of them of a defense nature, rather than any deep-seated conviction that the world would one day belong to them.

The Limits of American Power.   Soviet power confronted the West with continuing pressures against its unity, its prestige, and even its security. The challenge did not rest in communism "and the governments its controls," as Mr. Dulles often insisted, for the Communist governments of Poland and Yugoslavia were not hostile to the United States at all. The danger centered in the persistence of big nation rivalry. Russian policy pursued primarily its long-standing intention of establishing the largest possible hegemony for that nation in Eastern and Southeastern Europe. Amid the revolutions of Asia and Africa it sought, in addition, the political retreat of the West. What made the Soviet Union more threatening than in the past was not its ideology, but its relative power to achieve its goals. But if basic Soviet purpose was traditional, it still required more than spiritual strength to contain it within its historic precedents. Even this limited objective was vastly more dangerous than the rhetoric of world conquest and crusades for liberation suggested. The persistent effort to anchor American purpose to non-military devices encouraged the nation to underestimate the means required to preserve the West's precarious status in world affairs.

Unfortunately the military containment of Russia and China failed to achieve the vague but grandiose expectations attached to it. The moral and physical power required to frustrate Soviet intention proved to be illusive indeed. The search for military superiority through the creation of weapons of mass destruction brought no dilemma of the postwar era nearer settlement on Western terms. Much of the lack of realism in the national effort to counter the Soviet challenge stemmed from the general assumptions that the existence of thermonuclear weapons rendered war either impossible or so destructive that it would destroy civilization itself. The popular doctrine that war had been eliminated seemed to guarantee the time required for freedom to achieve its ultimate triumph over Communist tyranny. Meanwhile it encouraged the nation to live dangerously, to neglect its diplomacy, to respond to every threat of Communist expansion with "brinkmanship." At the same time the conviction that war could not be limited, or a nuclear war survived, ruled out the need of planning the conduct of future war to its conclusion, of maintaining conventional forces powerful enough to contain limited aggression with chemical explosives alone, of preparing for civil defense. Together these conclusions reduced military requirements to the mere possession of nuclear weapons and the means of their delivery. They satisfied the traditional American concern with tax reduction without forcing any diminution of national expectations. And they permitted the nation to ignore the sword of Damocles that hung over it, for there was no guarantee that war would not return to the world through deliberate attack, accident, or provocation.

Every trend of the fifties warred on the old bipolar concept of international power and weakened the Western alliance. England and France, no longer dependent on the United States for their existence, reasserted their former independent courses in world affairs. Charles de Gaulle, possessing his own atomic weapons, calmly defied the will of NATO. Germany and Japan, despite their verbal devotion to established military arrangements, threatened increasingly to move out on their own. Long-range missile development weakened the mutual interest of the United States and its Allies in the maintenance of European bases. The growing vulnerability of this nation to direct nuclear attack undermined much of Europe's confidence in the willingness of the American people to involve themselves in a European war. Somehow the United States seemed much more reliable when it was less vulnerable. The burgeoning concern of Europeans with their own nuclear arsenals reflected in some measure their conviction that they required their own deterrents against Soviet aggression.

The Failure of Peace. This nation's selfless search for order in world affairs could not sustain the gratitude of a troubled world. Its declining prestige stemmed less from the failure to match the Soviet achievements in space than from the failure to understand its own interests or the limits of its power. What undermined the world's confidence in American purpose was the habit of the nation's leaders to identify its ambitions with the cause of humanity and to turn every anti-Soviet maneuver into a mammoth crusade against the forces of darkness, with history hanging in the balance. The constant thunder of "liberation," "rollback," and "massive retaliation" confused and terrified the nation's friends more than it did its enemies. The persistent jabbing out in all directions, without regard to the forces involved, illustrated the plight of attempting to hold far-flung lines which Soviet and Chinese power rendered untenable. The conviction that everything was its business scarcely permitted the nation to judge when and how in any disturbance its interests were involved.

American leadership recognized the world's need for some evolution toward a stable peace. President Eisenhower declared repeatedly that "we will always go the extra mile with anyone on earth if it will bring us nearer a genuine peace." Despite his sincere devotion to the cause of peace, the President really could not lead the way toward any cold war settlement. Having agreed with Soviet leaders on the need of peace at the Geneva Summit Conference of July, 1955, he refused a month later to accept "a status quo in which we find injustice to many nations." On the following day Vice President Nixon demanded that the Russians dismantle the Iron Curtain, free the satellites, and unite Germany and Korea under free elections. At the Foreign Ministers' Conference in October, 1955, Mr. Dulles refused emphatically to accept Europe's status quo as the basis of negotiation. Nor did the demands of official Washington recede at any time during the next half decade. The President and his advisors had simply promised too much. They could make peace only on their own terms.

For that reason the President's specific proposals always substituted procedure for political settlement. In his message to Congress in January, 1958, for example, Mr. Eisenhower declared it essential that the world translate its desire for peace into action. The works of peace which the President then sought comprised the breaking down of unnatural barriers between nations, international cooperation in projects of human welfare, programs of science for peace, disarmament, and the establishment of a body of world law which would defend the strong against the weak and affirm the equality of nations. Actually all such proposals, uttered in the name of peace, promised no progress toward the organization of peace at all. For nowhere did they include the fundamental necessity of coming to terms, without conceding what belonged to the West, with the postwar status of Russia and China in world affairs.

This neglect of diplomacy amid a growing weariness with the cold war eventually forced both Mr. Eisenhower and Mr. Khrushchev to introduce high-level summitry and tourism as permanent rituals in international life. These were the only means remaining whereby responsible leaders could assure a drifting world that it was not drifting toward war. Unfortunately these procedures were developed in lieu of diplomacy; they reduced peacemaking to pure symbolism. Were settlement the real objective, it could have been obtained more cheaply and efficiently through established diplomatic procedures. Mr. Eisenhower's tours of 1959 and 1960, for example, equated the cause of peace with the enthusiasm of the crowds which greeted him abroad. Yet it was this nation's relations with the governments of Moscow and Peiping, not the crowds of New Delhi, Paris, and Taipei, that mattered. Despite all this apparent search for peace, the fundamental issues that plagued the world dragged on, unfaced and unsettled.

— 7 —

CONCLUSION: THE PROBLEM OF CHOICE

The Nature of American Foreign Policy, 1945-1960. Measured by the limits of national power, American foreign policy served the country well during the first fifteen years of the postwar era. United States leadership, both Democratic and Republican, accepted the warning of Winston Churchill that the Soviet Union, heavily armed and traditionally aggressive, posed a danger to Western security. If those who determined national policy never agreed on the character and extent of the Russian threat, they chose to build and maintain the Atlantic Alliance as the surest guarantee against Soviet expansion and the recurrence of war. That Europe remained remarkably stable through fifteen years of sometimes bitter disagreement and tension must be attributed in large measure to the national effort of the American people. The repeated acceptance of change in the Afro-Asian world, seldom in accordance with this nation's will, was not in itself a measure of failure. Soviet gains in the turbulent subcontinents were decidedly limited; none of them challenged the vital interests of the United States. Through fifteen years of crises neither side in the cold war experienced any major gains or losses.

This relative stability in the balance of power demonstrated the need as well as the feasibility of coexistence between East and West. Fifteen years of continuous conflict illustrated repeatedly the finite character of both American and Soviet strength. But at no time between 1945 and 1960 did United States officials confine this nation's intentions abroad to the obvious limits of the power at their disposal. The language of American diplomacy, admirably designed to reassure a citizenry at home, promised no less than the gradual erosion, before the superior appeal of freedom, of those forces in the world that defied American purpose (a purpose identified generally with the exclusion of Communist influence from international politics). Such broad ideological goals, while popular in themselves, eliminated the considerable power of the United States from any precise role in guiding its diplomacy. It was never made clear how any acceptable national effort could extend the base of freedom around the globe or even curtail the power and ambition of either of the nation's major cold war antagonists. Thus United States policy in 1960 existed at two levels. Whereas day-to-day decisions permitted the Republic to coexist with the U.S.S.R. on terms that were generally satisfactory, the national preoccupation with goals of universal freedom and justice denied that coexistence with communism was an acceptable arrangement at all.

The American Dilemma: Principle vs. the National Interest. This clear discrepancy between the nation's transcendent mission and its limited authority repudiated the historic principle that external objectives be circumscribed by available means. This defiance of diplomatic tradition did not pass unchallenged. One question was fundamental to all serious discussion of American foreign policy after 1945: What was the nation attempting to defend? Or phrased in more popular terms: From what was it refusing to retreat? The problem was crucial, for the national leadership, in assigning diplomacy the vague task of deflating the Communist structure, never distinguished between the United States as a nation and the American way of life as objects to be safeguarded. A nation and its ideology are not synonymous. One is a geographical, economic, political, and military entity; the other is a concept that resides in the minds of men. When the two converge, as indeed they may, one policy can serve them both; when they diverge, the country must make a choice. In resolving the inescapable dilemma of choice in its relations with the Soviet bloc, American leadership in large measure placed the nation's destiny on the altar of its principles, assuming that the United States, with its vast resources, would take care of itself. To John Foster Dulles, for example, the Republic during his secretaryship was protecting both its security and its principles. But of these, he declared repeatedly, the principles came first.

Those who attributed to this choice not only the vagueness in the American response but also much of the failure in cold war diplomacy preferred that the country employ its limited resources in defense of its vital interests, convinced that the American way had meaning only to the extent that it was identified with a vigorous and successful nation. Until the United States separated its interests from its aspirations, there was no assurance that it could prevent miscalculation on the part of its rivals or assure a troubled world that it would never initiate war except in defense of clearly defined and reasonable national goals.

Many writers, accepting the historic notion that a nation's authority is limited by its physical power, doubted after 1945 that the expected triumph of Western principles, and the consequent destruction of Communist power, would occur. For that reason they could discover no genuine alternative but war to a *modus vivendi* with the Soviet bloc. Moreover, they regarded coexistence a hopeful arrangement. Except at Berlin, the vital interests of East and West were not in apparent conflict. The world, for all its tension, had experienced no decided shifts in the balance of power. Most lines of demarcation had been well established through tradition if not diplomatic agreement; few, it seemed, could be tampered with without setting off a war. The United States had actually coexisted with the Kremlin, the Peiping regime, and the satellite empire for over a decade—a decade of unprecedented material progress and almost untrammeled freedom. The nation had demonstrated its capacity to maintain the status quo where it seemed essential; it had not demonstrated any power—moral, economic, or military—to alter it appreciably. If great changes occurred within the satellites, Russia, or China in the direction of American ambition, it would not be because the United States so willed it, but because massive forces present in those areas so willed it. The West, it seemed, could have what it needed; it could not have much more.

That illusive balance between ends and means required for the diplomatic acceptance and successful preservation of a state of coexistence, seemed to demand in 1960 added strength as well as reduced ambitions. If a multi-purpose defense structure, including adequate conventional forces, entailed a heavier drain on the treasury, it was still cheaper by far than one day of thermonuclear war. But whatever the size of the country's military establishment, its peacetime usefulness hinged on an admission that the persistent overexpectation of the fifties, which had no counterpart in actual provision for war, had not served the West's genuine interests or even its principles. The obvious discrepancy between words and actions in every European and Asian crisis tended to challenge the seriousness of the national response. Liberation, as the London *Economist* asserted, meant the risk of war or it meant nothing. If Western survival required the liberation of the satellites and the unification of Germany under free elections, why did the nation not prepare itself to pay the necessary military price? If such objectives were not worth that price, why had their fulfillment been made the *sine qua non* of coexistence?

There were many unrecognized arrangements in the world which defied the principle of self-determination; no American took any pleasure at their existence. But some observers pointed to the nation's lack of power, and therefore of obligation, to serve mankind in general. It seemed apparent after 1945 that any decided attempt to eliminate from the world those factors which appeared immoral would terminate in the destruction of the considerable good that still remained. Some writers wondered if the verbal acceptance of an obligation to universal freedom, when specific policies were not created to assure its fulfillment, was even moral. Such commitments saved no one and rendered improbable the settlement of any cold war issues through negotiation alone. They misled friend and foe alike, for the persistent tendency to overpromise meant that someone would be disillusioned in every crisis.

There remained in 1960 some consequential lessons of history. For a century the repeated involvement of the United States in war had resulted from a well-established pattern of diplomatic behavior. Prior to every involvement the nation's leadership had refused to accept certain conditions beyond its control as immoral, yet not sufficiently dangerous to the national interest to necessitate any preparation for war. Refusing to resolve these challenges to principle either through diplomacy or a show of force, the country drifted without benefit of genuine policy until the fundamental decisions between peace and war were made, to a large extent, by others. Perhaps the perennial absence of national concern at this pattern of faltering leadership in time of crisis was understandable, for in every conflict the country seemed to achieve gains commensurate with the price of victory. Never was this more true than for the Civil War itself. Unfortunately a century later the United States no longer possessed the advantages of geographic insulation and industrial superiority which had always assured victory in the past. Yet the nation, with its interests ill-defined in a general crusade for self-determination, entered a new period of drift after World War II not unlike that of the thirties. Thereafter through fifteen years of cold war experience American leadership could not prepare the country to accept either the necessity of coexistence with those forces which challenged its principles or the price required for dismantling the world which it could not accept.

Part II

DOCUMENTS

— Document No. 1 —

CORDELL HULL'S RADIO ADDRESS, APRIL 9, 1944[1]

Perhaps no speech of the war years illustrates better the purposes and hopes of American leadership in fighting the war than Hull's speech over the Columbia Broadcasting System on April 9, 1944. To Hull the United States, with its Allies, was seeking victory to establish a world based on the principles of the Atlantic Charter. Only the necessity of defeating Germany and Japan permitted the Secretary of State to obscure the incompatibility between the purpose of achieving Soviet compliance with this peacetime goal and the demonstrated Russian desire to maintain some tangible evidence of victory.

✁   ✁   ✁

. . . In talking about foreign policy it is well to remember, as Justice Holmes said, that a page of history is worth a volume of logic. There are three outstanding lessons in our recent history to which I particularly wish to draw your attention. In the first place, since the outbreak of the present war in Europe, we and those nations who are now our allies have moved from relative weakness to strength. In the second place, during that same period we

[1] Leland M. Goodrich and Marie J. Carroll (eds.), *Documents on American Foreign Relations, July 1943-June 1944* (Vol. VI, Boston, 1945), pp. 25-35.

in this country have moved from a deep-seated tendency toward separate action to the knowledge and conviction that only through unity of action can there be achieved in this world the results which are essential for the continuance of free peoples. And, thirdly, we have moved from a careless tolerance of evil institutions to the conviction that free governments and Nazi and Fascist governments cannot exist together in this world because the very nature of the latter requires them to be aggressors and the very nature of free governments too often lays them open to treacherous and well-laid plans of attack. . . .

The allied strength has now grown to the point where we are on the verge of great events. Of military events I cannot speak. It is enough that they are in the hands of men who have the complete trust of the American people. We await their development with absolute confidence. But I can and should discuss with you what may happen close upon the heels of military action.

As I look at the map of Europe, certain things seem clear to me. As the Nazis go down to defeat they will inevitably leave behind them in Germany and the satellite states of southeastern Europe a legacy of confusion. It is essential that we and our Allies establish the controls necessary to bring order out of this chaos as rapidly as possible and do everything possible to prevent its spread to the German-occupied countries of eastern and western Europe while they are in the throes of reestablishing government and repairing the most brutal ravages of the war. If confusion should spread throughout Europe it is difficult to overemphasize the seriousness of the disaster that may follow. Therefore, for us, for the world, and for the countries concerned, a stable Europe should be an immediate objective of allied policy.

Stability and order do not and cannot mean reaction. Order there must be to avoid chaos. But it must be achieved in a manner which will give full scope to men and women who look forward, men and women who will end Fascism and all its works and create the institutions of a free and democratic way of life.

We look with hope and with deep faith to a period of great democratic accomplishment in Europe. Liberation from the German yoke will give the peoples of Europe a new and magnificent opportunity to fulfill their democratic aspirations, both in building democratic political institutions of their own choice and in achieving the social and economic democracy on which political democracy must rest. It is important to our national interest to encourage the establishment in Europe of strong and progressive popular governments, dedicated like our own to improving the social welfare of the people as a whole—governments which will join the common effort of nations in creating the conditions of lasting peace and in promoting the expansion of production, employment, and the exchange and consumption of goods, which are the material foundations of the liberty and welfare of all peoples. . . .

However difficult the road may be, there is no hope of turning victory into enduring peace unless the real interests of this country, the British Commonwealth, the Soviet Union, and China are harmonized and unless they agree and act together. This is the solid framework upon which all future policy and international organization must be built. It offers the fullest opportunity for the development of institutions in which all free nations may participate democratically, through which a reign of law and morality may arise, and through which the material interests of all may be advanced. But without an enduring understanding between these four nations upon their fundamental purposes, interests, and obligations to one another, all organizations to preserve peace are creations on paper and the path is wide open again for the rise of a new aggressor. . . .

The road to agreement is a difficult one, as any man knows who has ever tried to get two other men, or a city council, or a trade gathering, or a legislative body, to agree upon anything. Agreement can be achieved only by trying to understand the other fellow's point of view and by going as far as possible to meet it.

Although the road to unity of purpose and action is long and difficult we have taken long strides upon our way. The Atlantic Charter was proclaimed by the President and the Prime Minister of Great Britain in August 1941. Then, by the Declaration of the United States of January 1, 1942, these nations adopted the principles of

the Atlantic Charter, agreed to devote all their resources
to the winning of the war, and pledged themselves not to
conclude a separate armistice or peace with their common
enemies.

After that came the declaration signed at Moscow on
October 30, 1943. Here the four nations who are carrying
and must carry the chief burden of defeating their enemies
renewed their determination by joint action to achieve
this end. But they went farther than this and pledged cooperation with one another to establish at the earliest
practicable date, with other peace-loving states, an effective international organization to maintain peace and
security, which in principle met with overwhelming nonpartisan approval by the Congress in the Connally and
Fulbright resolutions.

Further steps along the road of united allied action
were taken at the conference at Cairo, where the President
and Mr. Churchill met with Generalissimo Chiang Kai-
shek, and at the conference at Tehran, where they met
with Marshal Stalin. At Tehran the three Allies fighting
in Europe reached complete agreement on military plans
for winning the war and made plain their determination
to achieve harmonious action in the period of peace. That
concert among the Allies rests on broad foundations of
common interests and common aspirations, and it will endure. The Tehran declaration made it clear also that in
the tasks of peace we shall welcome the cooperation and
active participation of all nations, large and small, which
wish to enter into the world family of democratic nations.

The Cairo declaration as to the Pacific assured the
liquidation of Japan's occupations and thefts of territory
to deprive her of the power to attack her neighbors again,
to restore Chinese territories to China, and freedom to the
people of Korea. . . .

There has been discussion recently of the Atlantic
Charter and of its application to various situations. The
Charter is an expression of fundamental objectives toward
which we and our Allies are directing our policies. It
states that the nations accepting it are not fighting for the
sake of aggrandizement, territorial or otherwise. It lays
down the common principles upon which rest the hope of
liberty, economic opportunity, peace, and security through

international cooperation. It is not a code of law from which detailed answers to every question can be distilled by painstaking analysis of its words and phrases. It points the direction in which solutions are to be sought; it does not give solutions. It charts the course upon which we are embarked and shall continue. That course includes the prevention of aggression and the establishment of world security. The Charter certainly does not prevent any steps, including those relating to enemy states, necessary to achieve these objectives. What is fundamental are the objectives of the Charter and the determination to achieve them. . . .

We have found no difference of opinion among our Allies that the organization and purposes of the Nazi state and its Japanese counterpart, and the military system in all of its ramifications upon which they rest, are, and by their very nature must be, directed toward conquest. There was no disagreement that even after the defeat of the enemy there will be no security unless and until our victory is used to destroy these systems to their very foundation. The action which must be taken to achieve these ends must be, as I have said, agreed action. We are working with our Allies now upon these courses.

The conference at Moscow . . . established the European Advisory Commission, which is now at work in London upon the treatment of Germany. Out of these discussions will come back to the governments for their consideration proposals for concrete action.

Along with arrangements by which nations may be secure and free must go arrangements by which men and women who compose those nations may live and have the opportunity through their efforts to improve their material condition. As I said earlier, we will fail indeed if we win a victory only to let the free peoples of the world, through any absence of action on our part, sink into weakness and despair. The heart of the matter lies in action which will stimulate and expand production in industry and agriculture and free international commerce from excessive and unreasonable restrictions. . . .

I shall not on this occasion be able to explain the work which has been done—and it is extensive—in these fields. In many of them proposals are far advanced toward the

stage of discussion with members of the Congress prior
to formulation for public discussion.

I hope, however, that I have been able in some measure
to bring before you the immensity of the task which lies
before us all, the nature of the difficulties which are involved, and the conviction and purpose with which we are
attacking them. Our foreign policy is comprehensive, is
stable, and is known of all men. As the President has said,
neither he nor I have made or will make any secret agreement or commitment, political or financial. The officials
of the Government have not been unmindful of the responsibility resting upon them, nor have they spared either
energy or such abilities as they possess in discharging that
responsibility. . . .

— Document No. 2 —

SPEECH OF CAPTAIN THORNEYCROFT IN THE BRITISH HOUSE OF COMMONS, FEBRUARY 28, 1945 [2]

Captain Thorneycroft, addressing the House of Commons on the subject of the Yalta Agreement, recognized what many American leaders refused to do—that the control of Eastern Europe had passed to the Soviets and that the Yalta Agreement was the best settlement possible. For him the maintenance of the alliance was more important than a struggle over Poland.

1   1   1

I believe that the decisions which were arrived at at the Crimea Conference and, in particular, the decision relating to Poland, were wise decisions which were taken in circumstances of very considerable difficulty. . . . As I have said, each of these heads of States was laying down the future path we were likely to follow in our foreign affairs, and on the choice of that road hangs the issue as to whether, in another 30 years, we shall have another war or peace. We have had to face issues of this kind before. They are horribly familiar.

Twenty-five years ago, towards the end of another war, we were also discussing the rights of small Powers, and the future organisation of peace, and I have no doubt that on that occasion we made many mistakes. At any rate, it is certain that in the unhappy years which followed we made mistakes, and none of us wants to reiterate the sad

² *Parliamentary Debates, House of Commons, Fifth Series,* Vol. 408, pp. 1454-61.

story of the path which led a Germany not totally disarmed to the reoccupation of the Rhineland, through Munich and Berchtesgaden, and eventually to war. It seems to me, looking at that past history, that the mistakes we made were not so much on detailed decisions of British statesmen trying to stave off disaster, as in the failure to face the real issues in foreign policy at an early enough date. . . . If we are to enter in another period in which the facts of a certain situation in foreign affairs are to be tortured to fit into some international document to which we have affixed our signature we shall enter upon a course which must eventually lead us to another war, a war in which we shall have very few friends, and a process which will be detrimental to British honour. . . .

I do not believe that this Crimea Conference is the first milestone in the downward path. I do not believe that this Polish settlement is a betrayal of Poland or of British honour. Polish and British interests are to a large extent the same. We each have an interest to see that no one Power should dominate the whole of Europe. But the first British interest that we have is to finish this war at the earliest possible date. It is common ground that the German people have, or had, until recently, only one hope, and that was that the Allies would fall out among themselves. If the decisions taken at the Crimea Conference are supported by this House then that hope will be finally dispelled. . . .

I do not want to elaborate on the international organisation, because I think that that would be out of order now, but I think that when it is said that Poland can rely upon an international organisation to see that this settlement is kept she is entitled to ask what that international organisation will amount to. If there is one lesson we have learned from the history of the last quarter of a century it is that an international organisation, unless backed up by military power, is both valueless and dangerous. Under the Yalta Agreement, we are committed to the provision of an occupation Army on German soil. We are committed to a number of agreements which, if not world wide, will be very wide indeed. I presume that the Government have gone into the logistics of this matter. I presume that they have estimated what Forces will be required in order to carry out these commitments. The next step which is required is not so much a decision on voting rights at San Francisco as a forthright statement from this Government, the National Government, to the British people as to what sacrifices will be involved. What is required is a statement as to the Forces we shall have to raise in order to carry out what we shall have to do, and a clear statement as to whether compulsory military service will be necessary, as I think it will be. . . .

I believe the settlement we have reached with regard to Poland is the best settlement we could have got. It is worth while remembering that in statesmanship and politics what counts is not the art of getting what is best, but the art of getting what is possible. I concede at once—and this may be embarrassing for the Government—that I do not regard the Polish settlement as an act of justice. It may be right or wrong, it may be wise or foolish, but at any rate it is not justice as I understand the term. It is not the sort of situation in which you get two parties to a dispute putting their case forward in front of a disinterested body and in which the strength and power of one of the parties is never allowed to weigh in the balance. The sooner we recognize that we are a long way from that sort of thing happening the better.

The Government had two choices only. They could have postponed the issue. . . . They could have said, "No, we want this submitted to arbitration. We cannot do anything without the consent of the London Polish Government." No one knows what would happen in those circumstances, but one can safely say that it is unlikely that there would in any circumstance be a free, independent and democratic Poland. The Red Army is in occupation of that country and the Lublin Committee is in control. . . . The second course that they could adopt was to make the best settlement they could and impose it deliberately on the Poles. They have done that. They have bargained the Eastern frontier for the chance of a free Government of Poland within the new frontier. . . . We have encouraged the London Polish Government to negotiate, and have criticised them because they did not negotiate very well. We have told them they must make concessions, and then we have blamed them because they did not make concessions. I do not regard that as a sensible or an honourable course. I do not believe you can ask a Pole to decide to hand over a half of his country. I do not think it is a fair thing to ask any Pole to do. If they agreed to do that, they would divide Poland for a generation, perhaps for all time, into those who thought they were patriots and those who thought they were traitors. This is to perpetuate civil war. Nor could you ask the Poles as an act of policy to take a large slice of their powerful neighbouring State. It is a big decision to take from Germany the whole of East Prussia or the land up to the Oder. It is like taking Wales from England. That is a decision which must be taken by more powerful States. I do not believe that you save your honour in this matter by imposing on others the obligation of making a decision which you ought to make yourself.

I believe the real difficulty in which my hon. Friends find themselves is not so much Poland at all. I believe it is in the apparent conflict between documents like the Atlantic Charter, and the facts of the European situation. We talk to two different people in two different languages. In the East we are talking to the Russians. The Russians are nothing if not realists. I believe Marshal Stalin's motives are entirely honourable. I believe that the Russian Foreign Office is perhaps more in tune with the advice which would be given to the Tsars than to the potentates of the twentieth century. In such circumstances we talk in language not far removed from power politics. In the West we are faced by the Americans. They are nothing if not idealists. To them we talk in the polite language of the Atlantic Charter. Somehow or other we have to marry those two schools of thought. If I could persuade the Americans, particularly in the Middle West, to have something of the Russian realism in international relations, and persuade the Russians to have the idealism that exists on the East coast of America, we might get somewhere, but let us face the fact that the process will be a long and painful one. You do not move suddenly from a world in which there are international rivalries, into a world where there is international co-operation. It is the world that we are in that the Prime Minister has to deal with. We could not come back from Yalta with a Blue-print for a new

Utopia. The fundamental error into which my hon. Friends have fallen is this. The rights of small nations are not safeguarded by signing documents like the Atlantic Charter, and quarrelling with anyone who does not agree with your interpretation of them. The rights of small nations are safeguarded by a mixture of diplomacy and military power and, in using those things, you are liable to come into conflict with your friends. . . . The Government are trying to obtain a free, independent and democratic Poland, when the country is occupied by a foreign, though a friendly, Army belonging to a country which has not quite the same interpretation of what is free, independent and democratic as ourselves. . . . But throughout this process the Government have pursued a consistent course. They have sought by every means in their power to obtain from the wreck of Europe two independent and free States. To the Poles I would say that I believe this settlement gives them an opportunity of playing a part in the future of their country which they can never do from London. They should take that opportunity. To the Russians I would say that this is regarded as a test case. The proof of this pudding is in the eating. Russia has many friends in this country. On the decision and action that she takes in the coming weeks with regard to Poland will depend not only whether she keeps those friends but the whole future of co-operation between our two countries. As regards ourselves, I would say that this document provides what may be the basis of future peace. It will only be that, if we are prepared to face up to the sacrifices and the efforts which it involves and to recognize that those sacrifices and efforts are, indeed, worth while.

— Document No. 3 —

CHURCHILL'S SPEECH AT FULTON, MISSOURI, MARCH 5, 1946[3]

Winston Churchill was one of the first Western leaders to view Russia as a military threat. In his famous "Iron Curtain" speech at Fulton he suggested a military response comprising the creation of a joint United States-British military establishment. Churchill made no effort to analyze Soviet intentions, but he knew from experience that the possession of superior military power by one nation leads to aggression unless countered by opposing military power.

✓   ✓   ✓

. . . The United States stands at this time at the pinnacle of world power. It is a solemn moment for the American democracy. With primacy in power is also joined an awe-inspiring accountability to the future. As you look around you, you must feel not only the sense of duty done but also feel anxiety lest you fall below the level of achievement. Opportunity is here now, clear and shining, for both our countries. To reject it or ignore it or fritter it away will bring upon us all the long reproaches of the aftertime. It is necessary that constancy of mind, persistency of purpose and the grand simplicity of decision shall guide and rule the conduct of the English-speaking peoples in peace as they did in war. We must and I believe we shall prove ourselves equal to this severe requirement.

When American military men approach some serious situation they are wont to write at the head of their directive the words, "over-all strategic concept." There is wis-

[3] *Vital Speeches of the Day,* XII (March 15, 1946), pp. 329-32.

dom in this as it leads to clarity of thought. What, then, is the over-all strategic concept which we should inscribe today? It is nothing less than the safety and welfare, the freedom and progress of all the homes and families of all the men and women in all the lands. . . .

To give security to these countless homes they must be shielded from the two gaunt marauders—war and tyranny. We all know the frightful disturbance in which the ordinary family is plunged when the curse of war swoops down upon the bread winner and those for whom he works and contrives. The awful ruin of Europe, with all its vanished glories, and of large parts of Asia, glares in our eyes. When the designs of wicked men or the aggressive urge of mighty states dissolve, over large areas, the frame of civilized society, humble folk are confronted with difficulties with which they cannot cope. For them all is distorted, broken or even ground to pulp. . . . Our supreme task and duty is to guard the homes of the common people from the horrors and miseries of another war. . . .

I now come to the second danger which threatens the cottage home and ordinary people, namely tyranny. . . . It is not our duty at this time, when difficulties are so numerous, to interfere forcibly in the internal affairs of countries whom we have not conquered in war, but we must never cease to proclaim in fearless tones the great principles of freedom and the rights of man, which are the joint inheritance of the English-speaking world and which, through Magna Carta, the Bill of Rights, the habeas corpus, trial by jury and the English common law, find their most famous expression in the Declaration of Independence.

All this means that the people of any country have the right and should have the power by constitutional action, by free, unfettered elections, with secret ballot, to choose or change the character or form of government under which they dwell, that freedom of speech and thought should reign, that courts of justice independent of the executive, unbiased by any party, should administer laws which have received the broad assent of large majorities or are consecrated by time and custom. Here are the title deeds of freedom, which should lie in every cottage home. Here is the message of the British and American peoples to mankind. Let us preach what we practice and practice what we preach. . . .

Neither the sure prevention of war, nor the continuous rise of world organization will be gained without what I have called the fraternal association of the English-speaking peoples. This means a special relationship between the British Commonwealth and Empire and the United States. This is no time for generalities. I will venture to be precise. Fraternal association requires not only the growing friendship and mutual understanding between our two vast but kindred systems of society but the continuance of the intimate relationships between our military advisers, leading to common study of potential dangers, similarity of weapons and manuals of instruction and inter-change of officers and cadets at colleges. It should carry with it the continuance of the present facilities for mutual security by the joint use of all naval and air-force bases in the possession of either country all over the world. This would perhaps double the mobility of the American Navy and Air Force. . . .

A shadow has fallen upon the scenes so lately lighted by the Allied victory. Nobody knows what Soviet Russia and its Communist international organization intends to do in the immediate future, or what are the limits, if any, to their expansive and proselytizing tendencies. I have a strong admiration and regard for the valiant Russian people and for my war-time comrade, Marshal Stalin. . . . We understand the Russians need to be secure on her western frontiers from all renewal of German aggression. We welcome her to her rightful place among the leading nations of the world. Above all we welcome constant, frequent and growing contacts between the Russian people and our own people on both sides of the Atlantic. . . .

From Stettin in the Baltic to Trieste in the Adriatic, an iron curtain has descended across the Continent. Behind that line lie all the capitals of the ancient states of central and eastern Europe. Warsaw, Berlin, Prague, Vienna, Budapest, Belgrade, Bucharest, and Sofia, all these famous cities and the populations around them lie in the Soviet sphere and all are subject in one form or another, not only to Soviet influence but to a very high and increasing measure of control from Moscow. . . .

In front of the iron curtain which lies across Europe are other causes for anxiety. In Italy the Communist party is seriously hampered by having to support the Communist trained Marshal Tito's claims to former Italian territory at the head of the Adriatic. Nevertheless the future of Italy hangs in the balance. Again one cannot imagine a regenerated Europe without a strong France. All my public life I have worked for a strong France and I never lost faith in her destiny, even in the darkest hours. I will not lose faith now. However, in a great number of countries, far from the Russian frontiers and throughout the world, Communist fifth columns are established and work in complete unity and absolute obedience to the directions they receive from the Communist center. Except in the British Commonwealth and in this United States, where Communism is in its infancy, the Communist parties or fifth columns constitute a growing challenge and peril to Christian civilization. . . .

The outlook is also anxious in the Far East and especially in Manchuria. The agreement which was made at Yalta, to which I was a party, was extremely favorable to Soviet Russia, but it was made at a time when no one could say that the German war might not extend all through the summer and autumn of 1945 and when the Japanese war was expected to last for a further eighteen months from the end of the German war. . . .

On the other hand I repulse the idea that a new war is inevitable; still more that it is imminent. It is because I am so sure that our fortunes are in our own hands and that we hold the power to save the future, that I feel the duty to speak out now that I have an occasion to do so. I do not believe that Soviet Russia desires war. What they desire is the fruits of war and the indefinite expansion of their power and doctrines. But what we have to consider here today while time remains, is the permanent prevention of war and the establishment of conditions of freedom and democracy as rapidly as possible in all countries. Our difficulties and dangers will not be removed by closing our eyes to them. They will not be removed by mere waiting to see what happens; nor will they be relieved by a policy of appeasement. What is needed is a settlement and the longer this is delayed the more difficult it will be and the greater our dangers will become. From what I have seen of our Russian friends and allies during the war, I am convinced that there is nothing they admire so much as strength, and there is nothing for which they have less respect than for military weakness. For that reason the old doctrine of a balance of power is unsound. We cannot afford, if we can help it, to work on narrow margins, offering temptations to a trial of strength. If the western democracies stand together in strict adherence to the principles of the United Nations Charter, their influence for furthering these principles will be immense and no one is likely to molest them. If, however, they become divided or falter in their duty, and if these all-important years are allowed to slip away, then indeed catastrophe may overwhelm us all. . . .

If the population of the English-speaking commonwealth be added to that of the United States, with all that such co-operation implies in the air, on the sea and in science and industry, there will be no quivering, precarious balance of power to offer its temptation to ambition or adventure. On the contrary, there will be an overwhelming assurance of security. . . .

— Document No. 4 —

TRUMAN'S SPEECH TO CONGRESS, MARCH 12, 1947[4]

*In this noted speech, President Harry S. Truman pub-
licized the concept of a global, ideological struggle between the United States and the U.S.S.R. In his request for
economic and military aid for Greece and Turkey, he
divided the world into free nations and oppressed nations
and committed the United States to support all free governments struggling to maintain themselves against their
own minorities or external pressures.*

↗   ↗   ↗

. . . The United States has received from the Greek
Government an urgent appeal for financial and economic
assistance. Preliminary reports from the American Economic Mission now in Greece and reports from the American Ambassador in Greece corroborate the statement of
the Greek Government that assistance is imperative if
Greece is to survive as a free nation. I do not believe that
the American people and the Congress wish to turn a
deaf ear to the appeal of the Greek Government.

Greece is not a rich country. Lack of sufficient natural
resources has always forced the Greek people to work
hard to make both ends meet. Since 1940, this industrious,
peace loving country has suffered invasion, four years of
cruel enemy occupation, and bitter internal strife. . . .

The Greek Government has also asked for the assistance
of experienced American administrators, economists and
technicians to insure that the financial and other aid given
to Greece shall be used effectively in creating a stable and
self-sustaining economy and in improving its public administration.

[4] *The New York Times,* March 13, 1947.

The very existence of the Greek state is today threatened by the terrorist activities of several thousand armed men, led by Communists, who defy the Government's authority at a number of points, particularly along the northern boundaries. A commission appointed by the United Nations Security Council is at present investigating disturbed conditions in Northern Greece and alleged border violations along the frontiers between Greece on the one hand and Albania, Bulgaria, and Yugoslavia on the other.

Meanwhile, the Greek Government is unable to cope with the situation. The Greek Army is small and poorly equipped. It needs supplies and equipment if it is to restore the authority of the Government throughout Greek territory.

Greece must have assistance if it is to become a self-supporting and self-respecting democracy. The United States must supply that assistance. We have already extended to Greece certain types of relief and economic aid but these are inadequate. There is no other country to which democratic Greece can turn. No other nation is willing and able to provide the necessary support for a democratic Greek Government. . . .

Greece's neighbor, Turkey, also deserves our attention. The future of Turkey as an independent and economically sound state is clearly no less important to the freedom-loving peoples of the world than the future of Greece. The circumstances in which Turkey finds itself today are considerably different from those of Greece. Turkey has been spared the disasters that have beset Greece. And during the war, the United States and Great Britain furnished Turkey with material aid. Nevertheless, Turkey now needs our support. . . . I am fully aware of the broad implications involved if the United States extends assistance to Greece and Turkey, and I shall discuss these implications with you at this time.

One of the primary objectives of the foreign policy of the United States is the creation of conditions in which we and other nations will be able to work out a way of life free from coercion. This was a fundamental issue in the war with Germany and Japan. Our victory was won cver countries which sought to impose their will, and their way of life upon other nations.

To ensure the peaceful development of nations, free from coercion, the United States has taken a leading part in establishing the United Nations. The United Nations is designed to make possible lasting freedom and independence for all its members. We shall not realize our objectives, however, unless we are willing to help free people to maintain their free institutions and their national integrity against aggressive movements that seek to impose upon them totalitarian regimes. This is no more than a frank recognition that totalitarian regimes imposed on free peoples, by direct or indirect aggression, undermine the foundations of international peace and hence the security of the United States.

The peoples of a number of countries of the world have recently had totalitarian regimes forced upon them against their will. The Government of the United States has made frequent protests against coercion and intimidation, in violation of the Yalta Agreement, in Poland, Rumania and Bulgaria. I must also state that in a number of other countries there have been similar developments. At the present moment in world history nearly every nation must choose between alternative ways of life. The choice is too often not a free one.

One way of life is based upon the will of the majority, and is distinguished by free institutions, representative government, free elections, guarantees of individual liberty, freedom of speech and religion, and freedom from political oppression.

The second way of life is based upon the will of a minority forcibly imposed upon the majority. It relies upon terror and oppression, a controlled press and radio, fixed elections, and the suppression of personal freedoms.

I believe that it must be the policy of the United States to support free peoples who are resisting attempted subjugation by armed minorities or by outside pressures.

I believe that we must assist free peoples to work out their own destinies in their own way.

I believe that our help should be primarily through economic and financial aid which is essential to economic stability and orderly political processes.

The world is not static, and the status quo is not sacred. But we cannot allow changes in the status quo in violation of the Charter of the United Nations by such methods as coercion, or by such subterfuges as political infiltration. In helping free and independent nations to maintain their freedom, the United States will be giving effect to the principles of the Charter of the United Nations. . . .

Should we fail to aid Greece and Turkey in this fateful hour, the effect will be far reaching to the West as well as to the East. We must take immediate and resolute action. . . .

— Document No. 5 —

MARSHALL'S SPEECH AT HARVARD UNIVERSITY, JUNE 5, 1947[5]

In this speech Secretary of State George C. Marshall not only argued for an expanded economic aid program for Europe but also, with the advice of the Policy Planning Staff of the State Department, attempted to extricate American foreign policy from the ideological context to which the Truman Doctrine had consigned it. Marshall made it clear that United States economic aid, under the new program, would be aimed at poverty and economic dislocation, not at any ideology or nation.

     ✓   ✓   ✓

I need not tell you gentlemen that the world situation is very serious. That must be apparent to all intelligent people. I think one difficulty is that the problem is one

[5] Raymond Dennett and Robert K. Turner (eds.), *Documents on American Foreign Relations, January 1-December 31, 1947* (Vol. IX, Princeton, 1949), pp. 1-11.

of such enormous complexity that the very mass of the facts presented to the public by press and radio make it exceedingly difficult for the man in the street to reach a clear appraisement of the situation. Furthermore, the people of this country are distant from the troubled areas of the earth and it is hard for them to comprehend the plight and consequent reactions of the long-suffering peoples, and the effect of those reactions on their governments in connection with our efforts to promote peace in the world.

In considering the requirements for the rehabilitation of Europe, the physical loss of life, the visible destruction of cities, factories, mines and railroads was correctly estimated, but it has become obvious during recent months that this visible destruction was probably less serious than the dislocation of the entire fabric of European economy. For the past ten years conditions have been highly abnormal. . . . The breakdown of the business structure of Europe during the war was complete. Recovery has been seriously retarded by the fact that two years after the close of hostilities a peace settlement with Germany and Austria has not been agreed upon. But even given a more prompt solution of these difficult problems, the rehabilitation of the economic structure of Europe quite evidently will require a much longer time and greater effort than had been foreseen. . . .

The division of labor is the basis of modern civilization. At the present time it is threatened with breakdown. The town and city industries are not producing adequate goods to exchange with the food-producing farmer. Raw materials and fuel are in short supply. Machinery is lacking or worn out. The farmer or the peasant cannot find the goods for sale which he desires to purchase. So the sale of his farm produce for money which he cannot use seems to him an unprofitable transaction. . . . Meanwhile people in the cities are short of food and fuel. So the governments are forced to use their foreign money and credits to procure these necessities abroad. This process exhausts funds which are urgently needed for reconstruction. . . .

The truth of the matter is that Europe's requirements for the next three or four years of foreign food and other essential products—principally from America—are so much greater than her present ability to pay that she must have substantial additional help, or face economic, social and political deterioration of a very grave character. . . .

It is logical that the United States should do whatever it is able to do to assist in the return of normal economic health in the world, without which there can be no political stability and no assured peace. Our policy is directed not against any country or doctrine but against hunger, poverty, desperation and chaos. Its purpose should be the revival of a working economy in the world so as to permit the emergence of political and social conditions in which free institutions can exist. Such assistance, I am convinced, must not be on a piecemeal basis as various crises develop. Any assistance that this Government may render in the future should provide a cure rather than a mere palliative. Any government that is willing to assist in the task of recovery will find full cooperation, I am sure, on the part of the United States Government. Any government which maneuvers to block the recovery of other countries cannot expect help from us. Furthermore, governments, political parties or groups which seek to perpetuate human misery in order to profit therefrom politically or otherwise will encounter the opposition of the United States.

It is already evident that, before the United States Government can proceed much further in its efforts to alleviate the situation and help start the European world on its way to recovery, there must be some agreement among the countries of Europe as to the requirements of the situation and the part those countries themselves will take in order to give proper effect to whatever action might be undertaken by this Government. It would be neither fitting nor efficacious for this Government to undertake to draw up unilaterally a program designed to place Europe on its feet economically. This is the business of the Europeans. The initiative, I think, must come from Europe. . . . The program should be a joint one, agreed to by a number, if not all, European nations.

An essential part of any successful action on the part of the United States is an understanding on the part of the people of America of the character of the problem and the remedies to be applied. Political passion and prejudice should have no part. With foresight, and a willingness on the part of our people to face up to the vast responsibility which history has clearly placed upon our country, the difficulties I have outlined can and will be overcome.

— Document No. 6 —

ACHESON'S SPEECH IN WASHINGTON, APRIL 22, 1950[6]

This speech of Secretary of State Dean G. Acheson before the American Society of Newspaper Editors comprised a good summary of his concept of containment of the Soviet Union. He made it clear that he sought a settlement with Russia, not that country's destruction. He did not here or elsewhere enumerate any achievable conditions for such a settlement.

✓   ✓   ✓

I would like to discuss with you the thing that is most important to all of us: the well-being and happiness and security of the United States. I ask you to put aside, for the moment, all considerations that are less important, to forget all differences of opinion that are less than vital. . . .

We are faced with a threat—in all sober truth I say this —we are faced with a threat not only to our country but to the civilization in which we live and to the whole physical environment in which that civilization can exist. This threat is the principal problem that confronts the whole United States in the world today. . . .

[6] The Department of State, *Strengthening the Forces of Freedom: Selected Speeches and Statements of Secretary of State Acheson, February 1949-April 1950* (Washington, 1950), pp. 1-9.

There is no miracle that will make it disappear from the earth. Having recognized this truth, we need not for a moment be discouraged or downhearted. We have open to us, and we are now pursuing, many lines of action that will meet the challenge confronting us. May I mention six lines of action.

Our first line of action—and this seems to me the basis of all the others I shall discuss—is to demonstrate that our own faith in freedom is a burning and a fighting faith. We are children of freedom. We cannot be safe except in an environment of freedom. We believe in freedom as fundamentally as we believe anything in this world. We believe in it for everyone in our country. And we don't restrict this belief to freedom for ourselves. We believe that all people in the world are entitled to as much freedom, to develop in their own way, as we want ourselves. . . .

We must use every means we know to communicate the value of freedom to the four corners of the earth. Our message must go out through leaflets, through our free press, radio programs and films, through exchange of students and teachers with other countries, and through a hundred other ways. . . .

Thirdly, it is not enough that one should have a faith and should make that faith articulate. It is also essential that we, and those who think like us, should have the power to make safe the area in which we carry that faith into action. This means that we must look to our defenses. It means that we must organize our defenses wisely and prudently, with all the ingenuity and all the methods in which we are best versed to make ourselves strong.

Every element of promise is present in our situation. We have the ingenuity, we have the productive power, we have the determination, we have the resources. But this is not a subject on which I am competent to dwell at length. The President's chief advisers in this field are our Secretary of Defense and our service secretaries, in whom we can have complete faith and confidence.

Fourthly, beyond faith and preachment and defense there lies the necessity of translating all of these into terms of the daily lives of hundreds of millions of peoples who live in this free world of ours. I am talking about the effort we are now making to help create a better material life for ourselves and for other people in many parts of the world.

One part of this effort has to do with setting in operation again the great workshops of the free world. Since the end of the war we have worked steadily at this problem and we have had a vast measure of success. The chimneys of these factories are smoking again, raw materials are moving into them, finished goods are moving out. Hundreds of millions of people see the spector of insecurity in their daily lives being pushed further back. . . .

Now while we are helping to get workshops going—old and new—and to get people producing in Europe and other parts of the world, we have to do still another thing. And that is to develop a sensible system of trade to exchange the goods which are being and will be produced. . . .

We are going to have to make a great national effort, also, to get our own trade with the rest of the world into balance, to get out of the situation where we are selling abroad much more than we are buying and making up the difference out of the pockets of American taxpayers. Nobody here or abroad wants that situation to continue indefinitely. As part of the remedy we shall have to buy more from abroad, and that will demand a concerted national effort.

The fifth line of action is in the political field. In this political field we have so far only scratched the surface of what can be done to bring the free world closer together, to make it stronger and more secure and more effective.

There are many ways of organizing the free world for common action and many different opinions on how it should be done. But I think it is important in this hour of danger to concentrate our minds and our energies on using the machinery we have at hand, on expanding it and making it work. When you look over the field, you will see that we now have created a great deal of good machinery.

There is the whole machinery of the United Nations which we are continually learning to use more effectively.

Within the framework of the United Nations we have other machinery, like the North Atlantic Treaty and the Organization of American States.

The free nations of Europe have banded together in the Council of Europe, in the Marshall Plan organization, and in a smaller group known as the Western Union. We can work with all of these organizations. We can use whichever is best suited to accomplish a particular purpose. What we need to do is to expand the machinery we have, to improve it, to use it with boldness and imagination, and, when necessary, to supplement it with new machinery.

Now our program of action would not be complete if I did not go on to a sixth field, and that is the area of our relations with the Soviet Union and the countries that have fallen under Communist control. In this field, as in our relations with the free nations, we have the machinery of negotiation at hand. In the United Nations we have a dozen or more conference tables at which our differences could be thrashed out, where unfortunately the Soviet chair stands empty at the present time. We shall go on trying to find a common ground for agreement, not perfect or eternal agreement, but at least a better arrangement for living together in greater safety. . . .

We do not propose to subvert the Soviet Union. We shall not attempt to undermine Soviet independence. And we are just as determined that Communism shall not by hook or crook or trickery undermine our country or any other free country that desires to maintain its freedom. That real and present threat of aggression stands in the way of every attempt at understanding with the Soviet Union. For it has been wisely said that there can be no greater disagreement than when someone wants to eliminate your existence altogether.

If, as, and when that idea of aggression, by one means or another, can be ruled out of our relations with the Soviet Union, then the greatest single obstacle to agreement will be out of the way. As the results of our actions become clear and the free world becomes stronger, it will, I believe, become progressivly easier to get agreements with the Soviet Union. . . .

— Document No. 7 —

ACHESON'S SPEECH IN WASHINGTON, JANUARY 12, 1950[7]

Acheson's speech before the National Press Club comprised a complete statement of American Far Eastern policy at mid-century. This policy, the Secretary pointed out, was anchored to the assumption of a vast revolutionary upheaval blanketing the Orient. He defined the nation's defense commitment in the Far East, including specifically Japan, the Ryukyus, and the Philippines. Recognizing the force of the Asiatic upheaval, he warned that henceforth the fundamental decisions in Asia would lie in Asian hands.

✓   ✓   ✓

. . . I am frequently asked: Has the State Department got an Asian policy? And it seems to me that that discloses such a depth of ignorance that it is very hard to begin to deal with it. The peoples of Asia are so incredibly diverse and their problems are so incredibly diverse that how could anyone, even the most utter charlatan, believe that he had a uniform policy which would deal with all of them. On the other hand, there are very important similarities in ideas and in problems among the peoples of Asia and so what we come to, after we understand these diversities and these common attitudes of mind, is the fact that there must be certain similarities of approach, and there must be very great dissimilarities in action. . . .

There is in this vast area what we might call a develop-

[7] *The Department of State Bulletin,* January 23, 1950, pp. 111-119.

ing Asian consciousness, and a developing pattern, and this, I think, is based upon two factors. . . .

One of these factors is a revulsion against the acceptance of misery and poverty as the normal condition of life. Throughout all of this vast area, you have that fundamental revolutionary aspect in mind and belief. The other common aspect that they have is the revulsion against foreign domination. Whether that foreign domination takes the form of colonialism or whether it takes the form of imperialism, they are through with it. They have had enough of it, and they want no more. . . .

Now, may I suggest to you that much of the bewilderment which has seized the minds of many of us about recent developments in China comes from a failure to understand this basic revolutionary force which is loose in Asia. The reasons for the fall of the Nationalist Government in China are preoccupying many people. All sorts of reasons have been attributed to it. Most commonly, it is said in various speeches and publications that it is the result of American bungling, that we are incompetent, that we did not understand, that American aid was too little, that we did the wrong things at the wrong time. . . . Now, what I ask you to do is to stop looking for a moment under the bed and under the chair and under the rug to find out these reasons, but rather to look at the broad picture and see whether something doesn't suggest itself. . . .

What has happened in my judgment is that the almost inexhaustible patience of the Chinese people in their misery ended. They did not bother to overthrow this government. There was really nothing to overthrow. They simply ignored it. . . . They completely withdrew their support from this government, and when that support was withdrawn, the whole military establishment disintegrated. Added to the grossest incompetence ever experienced by any military command was this total lack of support both in the armies and in the country, and so the whole matter just simply disintegrated.

The Communists did not create this. The Communists did not create this condition. They did not create this revolutionary spirit. They did not create a great force which moved out from under Chiang Kai-shek. But they

were shrewd and cunning to mount it, to ride this thing
into victory and into power. . . .

Now, let me come to another underlying and important
factor which determines our relations and, in turn, our
policy with the peoples of Asia. That is the attitude of
the Soviet Union toward Asia, and particularly towards
those parts of Asia which are contiguous to the Soviet
Union, and with great particularity this afternoon, to
north China.

The attitude and interest of the Russians in north
China, and in these other areas as well, long antedates
communism. This is not something that has come out of
communism at all. It long antedates it. But the Communist
regime has added new methods, new skills, and new concepts to the thrust of Russian imperialism. This Commu-
nistic concept and techniques have armed Russian imperialism with a new and most insidious weapon of
penetration. Armed with these new powers, what is happening in China is that the Soviet Union is detaching
the northern provinces [areas] of China from China and
is attaching them to the Soviet Union. This process is
complete in outer Mongolia. It is nearly complete in
Manchuria, and I am sure that in inner Mongolia and in
Sinkiang there are very happy reports coming from Soviet
agents to Moscow. This is what is going on. It is the
detachment of these whole areas, vast areas—populated
by Chinese—the detachment of these areas from China
and their attachment to the Soviet Union.

I wish to state this and perhaps sin against my doctrine
of nondogmatism, but I should like to suggest at any
rate that this fact that the Soviet Union is taking the four
northern provinces of China is the single most significant,
most important fact, in the relation of any foreign power
with Asia.

What does that mean for us? It means something very,
very significant. It means that nothing that we do and
nothing that we say must be allowed to obscure the
reality of this fact. All the efforts of propaganda will not
be able to obscure it. The only thing that can obscure
it is the folly of ill-conceived adventures on our part which
easily could do so, and I urge all who are thinking about
these foolish adventures to remember that we must not

seize the unenviable position which the Russians have
carved out for themselves. We must not undertake to
deflect from the Russians to ourselves the righteous anger,
and the wrath, and the hatred of the Chinese people which
must develop. It would be folly to deflect it to ourselves.
We must take the position we have always taken—that
anyone who violates the integrity of China is the enemy
of China and is acting contrary to our own interest. That,
I suggest to you this afternoon, is the first and the greatest
rule in regard to the formulation of American policy
toward Asia.

I suggest that the second rule is very like the first.
That is to keep our own purposes perfectly straight, perfectly pure, and perfectly aboveboard and do not get them
mixed-up with legal quibbles or the attempt to do one
thing and really achieve another. . . .

What is the situation in regard to the military security
of the Pacific area, and what is our policy in regard to it?

In the first place, the defeat and the disarmament of
Japan has placed upon the United States the necessity of
assuming the military defense of Japan so long as that is
required, both in the interest of our security and in the
interests of the security of the entire Pacific area and, in
all honor, in the interest of Japanese security. We have
American—and there are Australian—troops in Japan. I
am not in a position to speak for the Australians, but I
can assure you that there is no intention of any sort of
abandoning or weakening the defenses of Japan and that
whatever arrangements are to be made either through
permanent settlement or otherwise, that defense must and
shall be maintained.

This defensive perimeter runs along the Aleutians to
Japan and then goes to the Ryukyus. We hold important
defense positions in the Ryukyu Islands, and those we will
continue to hold. In the interest of the population of the
Ryukyu Islands, we will at an appropriate time offer to
hold these islands under trusteeship of the United Nations.
But they are essential parts of the defensive perimeter of
the Pacific, and they must and will be held.

The defensive perimeter runs from the Ryukyus to the
Philippine Islands. Our relations, our defensive relations
with the Philippines are contained in agreements between

us. Those agreements are being loyally carried out and will be loyally carried out. Both peoples have learned by bitter experience the vital connections between our mutual defense requirements. We are in no doubt about that, and it is hardly necessary for me to say an attack on the Philippines could not and would not be tolerated by the United States. But I hasten to add that no one perceives the imminence of any such attack.

So far as the military security of other areas in the Pacific is concerned, it must be clear that no person can guarantee these areas against military attack. But it must also be clear that such a guarantee is hardly sensible or necessary within the realm of practical relationship.

Should such an attack occur—one hesitates to say where such an armed attack could come from—the initial reliance must be on the people attacked to resist it and then upon the commitments of the entire civilized world under the Charter of the United Nations which so far has not proved a weak reed to lean on by any people who are determined to protect their independence against outside aggression. But it is a mistake, I think, in considering Pacific and Far Eastern problems to become obsessed with military considerations. Important as they are, there are other problems that press, and these other problems are not capable of solution through military means. These other problems arise out of the susceptibility of many areas, and many countries in the Pacific area, to subversion and penetration. That cannot be stopped by military means.

The susceptibility to penetration arises because in many areas there are new governments which have little experience in governmental administration and have not become firmly established or perhaps firmly accepted in their countries. They grow, in part, from very serious economic problems. . . . In part this susceptibility to penetration comes from the great social upheaval about which I have been speaking. . . .

So after this survey, what we conclude, I believe, is that there is a new day which has dawned in Asia. It is a day in which the Asian peoples are on their own, and know it, and intend to continue on their own. It is a day in which the old relationships between east and west are

gone, relationships which at their worst were exploita-
tions, and which at their best were paternalism. That relationship is over, and the relationship of east and west
must now be in the Far East one of mutual respect and
mutual helpfulness. We are their friends. Others are their
friends. We and those others are willing to help, but we
can help only where we are wanted and only where the
conditions of help are really sensible and possible. So what
we can see is that this new day in Asia, this new day which
is dawning, may go on to a glorious noon or it may darken
and it may drizzle out. But that decision lies within the
countries of Asia and within the power of the Asian
people. It is not a decision which a friend or even an
enemy from the outside can decide for them.

— Document No. 8 —

DULLES' STATEMENT ON LIBERATION, JANUARY 15, 1953[8]

*John Foster Dulles first publicized his concept of libera-
tion in his article, "A Policy of Boldness," Life, May 19,
1952. This concept he then wrote into the Republican
platform of 1952. When he appeared before the Senate
Foreign Relations Committee the following January, prior
to becoming Secretary of State, he insisted that the liberation of China and the Soviet satellites could be achieved
without war or even revolution. Precisely how he hoped
to achieve this he never stated, either here or elsewhere.*

✓   ✓   ✓

[8] *Hearing before the Committee on Foreign Relations, United
States Senate, Eighty-Third Congress, First Session, on
the Nomination of John Foster Dulles, Secretary of State-
Designate, January 15, 1953* (Washington, 1953), pp. 5-6.

. . . The CHAIRMAN. I am particularly interested in something I read recently, to the effect that you stated you were not in favor of the policy of containment. I think you advocated a more dynamic or positive policy.

Can you tell us more specifically what you have in mind? . . . .

Mr. DULLES. There are a number of policy matters which I would prefer to discuss with the committee in executive session, but I have no objection to saying in open session what I have said before: namely, that we shall never have a secure peace or a happy world so long as Soviet communism dominates one-third of all of the peoples that there are, and is in the process of trying at least to extend its rule to many others.

These people who are enslaved are people who deserve to be free, and who, from our own selfish standpoint, ought to be free because if they are the servile instruments of aggressive despotism, they will eventually be welded into a force which will be highly dangerous to ourselves and to all of the free world.

Therefore, we must always have in mind the liberation of these captive peoples. Now, liberation does not mean a war of liberation. Liberation can be accomplished by processes short of war. We have, as one example, not an ideal example, but it illustrates my point, the defection of Yugoslavia, under Tito from the domination of Soviet communism. Well, that rule of Tito is not one which we admire, and it has many aspects of despotism, itself; but at least it illustrates that it is possible to disintegrate this present monolithic structure which, as I say, represents approximately one-third of all the people that there are in the world.

The present tie between China and Moscow is an unholy arrangement which is contrary to the traditions, the hopes, the aspirations of the Chinese people. Certainly we cannot tolerate a continuance of that, or a welding of the 450 million people of China into the servile instruments of Soviet aggression.

Therefore, a policy which only aims at containing Russia where it now is, is, in itself, an unsound policy; but it is a policy which is bound to fail because a purely defensive policy never wins against an aggressive policy. If our only policy is to stay where we are, we will be driven back. It is only by keeping alive the hope of liberation, by taking advantage of that wherever opportunity arises, that we will end this terrible peril which dominates the world, which imposes upon us such terrible sacrifices and so great fears for the future. But all of this can be done and must be done in ways which will not provoke a general war, or in ways which will not provoke an insurrection which would be crushed with bloody violence, such as was the case, for example, when the Russians instigated the Polish revolt, under General Bor, and merely sat by and watched them when the Germans exterminated those who were revolting.

It must be and can be a peaceful process, but those who do not believe that results can be accomplished by moral pressures, by the weight of propaganda, just do not know what they are talking about.

I ask you to recall the fact that Soviet communism, itself, has spread from controlling 200 million people some 7 years ago to controlling 800 million people today, and it has done that by methods of political warfare, psychological warfare and propaganda, and it has not actually used the Red Army as an open aggressive force in accomplishing that.

Surely what they can accomplish, we can accomplish. Surely if they can use moral and psychological force, we can use it; and, to take a negative defeatest attitude is not an approach which is conducive to our own welfare, or in conformity with our own historical ideas. . . .

— Document No. 9 —

DULLES' SPEECH IN NEW YORK, JANUARY 25, 1954[9]

This complete statement of Dulles' entire concept of foreign affairs was critical of the Truman policies because they had been piecemeal and had always left the initiative to the Kremlin. It was necessary, he said, for the United States to develop long-range policies which would protect the nation's security at reduced cost. He found the answer in "massive retaliation." But he went far beyond the assurance that the United States could prevent aggression simply by threatening to employ its weapons of mass destruction, for he promised that the time gained by preventing aggression would produce erosion within the enemy states and thus eventually give this nation a victory in the cold war. This speech thus tied the concept of massive retaliation to the concept of peaceful liberation. It not only promised ultimate victory but also promised it at little risk and at reduced expenditures.

✓   ✓   ✓

. . . We live in a world where emergencies are always possible, and our survival may depend upon our capacity to meet emergencies. Let us pray that we shall always have that capacity. But, having said that, it is necessary also to say that emergency measures—however good for the emergency—do not necessarily make good permanent policies. Emergency measures are costly; they are superficial; and they imply that the enemy has the initiative. They cannot be depended on to serve our long-time interests.

[9] *The Department of State Bulletin,* January 25, 1954, pp. 107-10.

This "long time" factor is of critical importance. The Soviet Communists are planning for what they call "an entire historical era," and we should do the same. . . .

In the face of this strategy, measures cannot be judged adequate merely because they ward off an immediate danger. It is essential to do this, but it is also essential to do so without exhausting ourselves.

When the Eisenhower administration applied this test, we felt that some transformations were needed. It is not sound military strategy permanently to commit U.S. land forces to Asia to a degree that leaves us no strategic reserves. It is not sound economics, or good foreign policy, to support permanently other countries; for in the long run, that creates as much ill will as good will. Also, it is not sound to become permanently committed to military expenditures so vast that they lead to "practical bankruptcy." . . . We need allies and collective security. Our purpose is to make these relations more effective, less costly. This can be done by placing more reliance on deterrent power and less dependence on local defensive power.

This is accepted practice so far as local communities are concerned. We keep locks on our doors, but we do not have an armed guard in every home. We rely principally on a community security system so well equipped to punish any who break in and steal that, in fact, would-be aggressors are generally deterred. That is the modern way of getting maximum protection at a bearable cost.

What the Eisenhower administration seeks is a similar international security system. We want, for ourselves and the other free nations, a maximum deterrent at a bearable cost.

Local defense will always be important. But there is no local defense which alone will contain the mighty landpower of the Communist world. Local defenses must be reinforced by the further deterrent of massive retaliatory power. A potential aggressor must know that he cannot always prescribe battle conditions that suit him. Otherwise, for example, a potential aggressor, who is glutted with manpower, might be tempted to attack in confidence that resistance would be confined to manpower. He might be tempted to attack in places where his superiority was decisive. . . .

But before military planning could be changed, the President and his advisers, as represented by the National Security Council, had to take some basic policy decisions. This has been done. The basic decision was to depend primarily upon a great capacity to retaliate, instantly, by means and at places of our choosing. Now the Department of Defense and the Joint Chiefs of Staff can shape our military establishment to fit what is *our* policy, instead of having to try to be ready to meet the enemy's many choices. . . . As a result, it is now possible to get, and share, more basic security at less cost.

Let us now see how this concept has been applied to foreign policy, taking first the Far East. In Korea this administration effected a major transformation. The fighting has been stopped on honorable terms. That was possible because the aggressor, already thrown back to and behind his place of beginning, was faced with the possibility that the fighting might, to his own great peril, soon spread beyond the limits and methods which he had selected. . . .

I have said in relation to Indochina that, if there were open Red Chinese armed aggression there, that would have "grave consequences which might not be confined to Indochina." I expressed last month the intention of the United States to maintain its position on Okinawa. This is needed to insure adequate striking power to implement the collective concept which I describe.

All of this is summed up in President Eisenhower's important statement of December 26. He announced the progressive reduction of the U.S. ground forces in Korea. He pointed out that U.S. military forces in the Far East will now feature "highly mobile naval, air and amphibious units"; and he said in this way, despite some withdrawal of land forces, the United States will have a capacity to oppose aggression "with even greater effect than heretofore.". . .

At the April meeting of the NATO Council, the United States put forward a new concept, now known as that of the "long haul." That meant a steady development of defensive strength at a rate which will preserve and not exhaust the economic strength of our allies and ourselves. This would be reinforced by the striking power of a strategic air force based on internationally agreed positions. . . .

There are still some strategic spots where the local governments cannot maintain adequate armed forces without some financial support from us. In these cases, we take the judgment of our military advisers as to how to proceed in the common interest. For example, we have contributed largely, ungrudgingly, and I hope constructively, to end aggression and advance freedom in Indochina. The technical assistance program is being continued, and we stand ready to meet nonrecurrent needs due to crop failures or like disasters. But, broadly speaking, foreign budgetary aid is being limited to situations where it clearly contributes to military strength. . . .

If we can deter such aggression as would mean general war, and that is our confident resolve, then we can let time and fundamentals work for us. We do not need self-imposed policies which sap our strength. . . . We intend that our conduct and example shall continue, as in the past, to show all men how good can be the fruits of freedom.

If we rely on freedom, then it follows that we must abstain from diplomatic moves which would seem to endorse captivity. That would, in effect, be a conspiracy against freedom. I can assure you that we shall never seek illusory security for ourselves by such a "deal." We do negotiate about specific matters but only to advance the cause of human welfare. . . .

If we persist in the courses I outline we shall confront dictatorship with a task that is, in the long run, beyond its strength. For unless it changes, it must suppress the human desires that freedom satisfies—as we shall be demonstrating. If the dictators persist in their present course, then it is they who will be limited to superficial successes, while their foundation crumbles under the tread of their iron boots. . . .

We can be sure that there is going on, even within Russia, a silent test of strength between the powerful rulers and the multitudes of human beings. Each individual no doubt seems by himself to be helpless in this struggle. But their aspirations in the aggregate make up a mighty force. There are signs that the rulers are bending to some of the human desires of their people. There are promises of more food, more household goods, more economic freedom.

That does not prove that the Soviet rulers have themselves been converted. It is rather that they may be dimly perceiving a basic fact, that is that there are limits to the power of any rulers indefinitely to suppress the human spirit. In that God-given fact lies our greatest hope. It is a hope that can sustain us. For even if the path ahead be long and hard, it need not be a warlike path; and we can know that at the end may be found the blessedness of peace.

— Document No. 10 —

ALASTAIR BUCHAN'S ARGUMENT FOR GRADUATED DETERRENCE, DECEMBER 1, 1955 [10]

After its formal announcement in January, 1954, the doctrine of "massive retaliation" was subjected to so much critical analysis by both British and American writers that even Mr. Dulles was forced to modify his original statement and bury some of the questions raised with an appeal to secrecy. Alastair Buchan, the English writer, here criticises the doctrine's ineffectiveness in preventing small wars, especially after the Russians achieved nuclear parity as recognized by the Geneva summit conference of July, 1955. To him the West required a "graduated deterrence"

[10] Alastair Buchan, "Toward A New Strategy of Graduated Deterrence," *The Reporter*, December 1, 1955, pp. 23-28. Copyright 1955 by The Reporter Magazine Company.

*which included conventional forces sufficient to discourage
even local war.*

✓   ✓   ✓

The achievements of the [Geneva] "summit" meeting
still stand. It is an immense gain that the United States and
Russia should recognize that each has the power to destroy the other, and should be able to make each other
understand that for no mere difference of ideology will
either risk bringing destruction upon itself. But to imagine,
as most of us were tempted to, that the acknowledgment
of a stranglehold upon each other's throats might lead to
the beginning of a more constructive relationship between
East and West, has proved for the moment at least to be
a delusion.

For the fallacy was that the Russians had decided that
they must negotiate and co-operate with the West because
a state of over-all military stalemate had been reached. In
fact what had been reached, as the Russians recognized
more clearly than we, was a state of strategic stalemate
that left them with the tactical initiative—a new freedom
to use their overwhelming superiority in the form of much
larger conventional forces than the West is prepared to
support, and to nibble away at the periphery of the free
world.

What the Foreign Ministers' conference demonstrated,
therefore, is that reliance on one strategic weapon—the
hydrogen bomb—is now outdated and that there is the
most urgent need to discuss some means by which the
West can make itself tactically stronger than it is today.
The words "massive retaliation" and "ultimate deterrent"
have a deceptive ring of effectiveness about them. . . .
To the extent that [the nuclear deterrent] has never been
put to the test of a Russian attack on any of the vital
strategic areas of the West, it has been successful. But as
a deterrent to minor aggression it has twice been com-
promised. In the winter of 1950 the United Nations decided that it would take the risk of losing the war in Korea
rather than see it develop into a general conflict with
Russia as a consequence of authorizing the United States
to retaliate with atomic weapons against Chinese interven-

tion. In 1954 the Eisenhower Administration decided that
it would accept the loss of Dienbienphu and northern
Vietnam rather than use the ultimate deterrent to arrest
the defeat of conventional forces in Indo-China.

There were sound reasons in each case for holding back,
but as Denis Healey, one of the ablest minds on foreign
affairs in the House of Commons, wrote in a recent issue
of *Encounter*: "It cannot be denied that the deterrent
value of atomic striking power has seriously depreciated
through the West's proved reluctance to use it. From the
experience of the last five years, it would appear that a
general threat of atomic retaliation may well invite the
Communists to probe western intentions by local military
adventures."

Moreover, if in recent years moral and political scruples
have prevented the United States from using its advantage
in nuclear weapons, it is even less likely that they will be
used when the West no longer has the advantage in atomic
weapons. . . .

For these reasons there has been growing in the last
year or so an increasingly influential body of opinion in
favor of what is called "graduated deterrence" or "measured retaliation." Though the solutions differ, the problem
to which they are addressed is the same: to redress the
tactical balance of power with Russia by demonstrating
our ability and readiness to oppose Communist aggression
wherever it is applied, without making an exchange of
hydrogen bombs the automatic concomitant of a resort
to force. More simply, the attempt should be made to develop out of the balance of force some rules of war for
the nuclear age so that war may be confined to the battlefield—in the interest of both sides.

The men trying to think their way through this problem
are not starry-eyed idealists. The best-known advocate of
graduated deterrence is Canadian Foreign Secretary Lester
Pearson, who in a lecture at Princeton last April delivered
a strong warning against the "all-or-nothing" habit of
thought on which massive retaliation with the hydrogen
bomb is based. . . . In Britain, which has more to lose
from a policy of massive retaliation than any other first-
class power, the most articulate exponent of graduated

deterrence is Rear Admiral Sir Anthony Buzzard, who until last year was director of naval intelligence at the Admiralty.

Admiral Buzzard's thesis is that in view of the continuing deadlock between East and West on disarmament and the growing dread of the hydrogen bomb, the West should seize the initiative "by announcing our future intention of pursuing the moral principle of never using more force than necessary." He wrote recently in the Manchester *Guardian*: "To this end we might declare a distinction between the tactical and strategic use of nuclear weapons. Tactical use, we might say, we consider as confined to atomic weapons and as excluding even these from targets in centres of population. Strategic use we might declare as including hydrogen weapons and any nuclear attack on targets in centres of population. Next, without being too specific, we might state generally that we would reserve strategic use as a last resort. Ultimately we might even renounce strategic use unless the aggressor resorted to it. . . . Such steps could be taken without waiting on any agreement with the Communists."

. . . The feasibility of a policy of graduated deterrence is not accepted at present by any western general staff (including SHAPE), nor by many people who are worried by the implications of massive retaliation. There are three main arguments against it.

The first is the soldier's—that a commander cannot confront the enemy with his hands tied and that he must have every available weapon at his disposal. This is the weakest of the three because the plain fact is that decision to use a weapon of the destructive power of the hydrogen bomb is, and must always remain, political. . . .

The second question is whether the deterrent, because of being graduated to the scale of the aggression, would lose some of its power to deter. This is a very hard question because it involves an assessment of whether, by the determined use of tactical atomic weapons, the West can compensate for the superiority of Russian land power without recourse to strategic bombing. On this the experts differ. The only thing that can be said is that at present the American stockpile of atomic weapons (though not necessarily hydrogen bombs) is much larger than the

Russian. If a clear decision to concentrate on tactical weapons could be taken, it is difficult to see why this lead could not be maintained.

Finally, there is the thorny problem of establishing and maintaining the distinction between "strategic" and "tactical" targets. As the London *Economist* has pointed out, ". . . the undertakings that would be given under a policy of graduated deterrence would not be absolute promises, but conditional ones. In view of the fog of war and the paramount importance of speed, could much reliance be placed on promises not to do something unless the other fellow did it first?" Moreover, while it might be possible—though by no means easy—to draw a distinction between civil and military targets in America or Russia, it would be much harder in crowded countries like Britain or Belgium. Even if an informal understanding could be established that in the event of war only targets in the "war zone," say fifty or a hundred miles behind the enemy's front lines, would be attacked with atomic weapons, would that prevent an attempt to destroy submarine bases in Russia? How can one distinguish between civil and military targets for cities like Portsmouth or San Diego that are centers of population and also great naval ports?

These are the arguments that restrain the military and diplomatic planners from exploring the subject further. But no matter whether generals or statesmen like it or not, the debate on the future of deterrence and retaliation will certainly grow in volume and importance. For under the stress of the nuclear arms race, the need is urgent to rid ourselves of that twentieth-century heresy "total war," and of the idea that the object of war is victory, not peace.

— Document No. 11 —

DULLES' DEFENSE OF U.S. CHINA POLICY, JUNE 28, 1957[11]

In this speech, delivered in San Francisco, Mr. Dulles repeated the rationale developed by American officials after 1952 to explain and defend American policy toward China. These arguments were molded into a pattern which never varied. For that reason one need read only one full defense of the policy of nonrecognition to grasp the full argumentation.

✓   ✓   ✓

. . . On the China mainland 600 million people are ruled by the Chinese Communist Party. That party came to power by violence and, so far, has lived by violence. It retains power not by will of the Chinese people but by massive, forcible repression. It fought the United Nations in Korea; it supported the Communist war in Indochina; it took Tibet by force. It fomented the Communist Huk rebellion in the Philippines and the Communists' insurrection in Malaya. It does not disguise its expansionist ambitions. It is bitterly hateful of the United States, which it considers a principal obstacle in the way of its path of conquest.

In the fact of this condition the United States has supported, morally and materially, the free nations of the Western Pacific and Southeast Asia. Our security treaties make clear that the violation of these nations by international communism would be considered as endangering our own peace and safety and that we would act accordingly. Together we constitute a goodly company and a stout bulwark against aggression.

[11] *The Department of State Bulletin*, July 15, 1957, pp. 91-95.

As regards China, we have abstained from any act to encourage the Communist regime—morally, politically, or materially. . . .

United States diplomatic recognition of Communist China would have the following consequences:

(1) The many mainland Chinese, who by Mao Tse-tung's own recent admission seek to change the nature of their government, would be immensely discouraged.

(2) The millions of overseas Chinese would feel that they had no Free China to which to look. Today increasing numbers of these overseas Chinese go to Free China to study. Six years ago there were less than 100 Chinese students from Southeast Asia and Hong Kong studying in Taiwan. Now there are nearly 5,000. . . .

If the United States recognized the Chinese Communist regime, many of the millions of overseas Chinese in free Asian countries would, reluctantly, turn to acceptance of the guiding direction of the Communist regime. This would be a tragedy for them; and it would imperil friendly governments already menaced by Chinese Communist subversion.

(3) The Republic of China, now on Taiwan, would feel betrayed by its friend. That Government was our ally in the Second World War and for long bore alone the main burden of the Far Eastern war. It had many tempting opportunities to compromise with the Japanese on terms which would have been gravely detrimental to the United States. It never did so. . . . We are honorbound to give our ally, to whom we are pledged by a mutual defense treaty, a full measure of loyalty.

(4) The free Asian governments of the Pacific and Southeast Asia would be gravely perplexed. They are not only close to the vast Chinese land mass, but geographically and, to some extent, politically, they are separated as among themselves. The unifying and fortifying influence is, above all, the spirit and resolution of the United States. If we seemed to waver and to compromise with communism in China, that would in turn weaken free Asia resistence to the Chinese Communist regime and assist international communism to score a great success in its program to encircle us.

United States recognition of Communist China would

make it probable that the Communist regime would obtain the seat of China in the United Nations. That would not be in the interest either of the United States or of the United Nations. . . . Should a regime which in 7 years has promoted five foreign or civil wars—Korea, Indochina, Tibet, the Philippines, and Malaya . . . be given a permanent seat, with veto power, in the body which under the charter has "primary responsibility for the maintenance of international peace and security"?

Communist Russia, with its veto power, already seriously limits the ability of the United Nations to serve its intended purposes. Were Communist China also to become a permanent, veto-wielding member of the Security Council, that would, I fear, implant in the United Nations the seeds of its own destruction. . . .

Trade with Communist China is not a normal trade. It does not provide one country with what its people want but cannot well produce for themselves, in exchange for what other people want but cannot well produce themselves. Trade with Communist China is wholly controlled by an official apparatus, and its limited amounts of foreign exchange are used to develop as rapidly as possible a formidable military establishment and a heavy industry to support it. . . .

We also doubt the value of cultural exchanges, which the Chinese Communists are eager to develop. They want this relationship with the United States primarily because, once that example were given, it would be difficult for China's close neighbors not to follow it. These free nations, already exposed to intense Communist subversive activities, could not have the cultural exchanges that the Communists want without adding greatly to their danger.

These are the considerations which argue for a continuance of our present policies. What are the arguments on the other side?

There are some who say that we should accord diplomatic recognition to the Communist regime because it has now been in power so long that it has won the *right* to that. That is not sound international law. Diplomatic recognition is always a privilege, never a right.

Of course, the United States knows that the Chinese Communist regime exists. We know that very well, for it has fought us in Korea. . . . For nearly 2 years we have been, and still are, dealing with it in an effort to free our citizens and to obtain reciprocal renunciations of force.

But diplomatic recognition gives the recognized regime valuable rights and privileges, and, in the world of today, recognition by the United States gives the recipient much added prestige and influence at home and abroad. . . .

Another argument beginning to be heard is that diplomatic recognition is inevitable, so why not now?

First, let me say emphatically that the United States need never succumb to the argument of "inevitability." We, with our friends, can fashion our own destiny. We do not accept the mastery of Communist forces. . . . The reality is that a governmental system which tolerates diversity has a long life expectancy, whereas a system which seeks to impose conformity is always in danger. That results from the basic nature of human beings. . . .

We always take into account the possibility of influencing the Communist regime to better ways if we had diplomatic relations with it, or if, without that, we had commercial and cultural contacts with it. But the experience of those who now recognize and deal with the Chinese Communist regime convinces us that, under present conditions, neither recognition, nor trade, nor cultural relations, nor all three, would favorably influence the evolution of affairs in China. The probable result, internally, would be the opposite of what we hope for. . . .

Do we see any chance that the potentially great Chinese nation, with its rich and ancient culture and wisdom, will again be able to play a constructive part in the councils of the nations? We confidently answer these questions in the affirmative. Our confidence is based on certain fundamental beliefs. One is a belief in the future of human freedom. . . .

We can confidently assume that international communism's rule of strict conformity is, in China as elsewhere, a passing and not a perpetual phase. We owe it to ourselves, our allies, and the Chinese people to do all that we can to contribute to that passing.

If we believed that this passing would be promoted by trade and cultural relations, then we would have such relations. If we believed that this passing would be promoted by our having diplomatic relations with the present regime, then we would have such relations. If we believed that this passing would be promoted by some participation of the present regime in the activities of the United Nations, then we would not oppose that.

We should be, and we are, constantly testing our policies, to be as certain as we can be that, in the light of conditions as they from time to time are, our policies shall serve the great purposes to which our Nation has been dedicated since its foundation—the cause of peace, justice, and human liberty. . . .

Many free nations seek to coordinate their foreign policies with ours. Such coordination is indeed indispensable if the free world is to have the cohesion needed to make it safe. But United States policies will never serve as rallying points for free peoples if the impression is created that our policies are subject to change to meet Communist wishes for no reason other than that communism does not want to change. If communism is stubborn for the wrong, let us be steadfast for the right.

The capacity to change is an indispensable capacity. Equally indispensable is the capacity to hold fast that which is good. Given those qualities, we can hopefully look forward to the day when those in Asia who are yet free can confidently remain free and when the people of China and the people of America can resume their long history of cooperative friendship.

— Document No. 12 —

KENNETH YOUNGER'S CRITIQUE OF U.S. CHINA POLICY, SEPTEMBER, 1957[12]

Among the many critiques of American China policy which appeared during the fifties, none were more perceptive than that of Kenneth Younger, a Laborite member of the House of Commons. Many of his arguments were as stereotyped as those offered in defense of the policy. But Mr. Younger, more than most American critics, was concerned with the effort of this nation to isolate mainland China diplomatically in the Orient, for he believed that all Asia would learn to live with China or become involved in war which would serve the interests of neither the West nor the countries of Asia.

✓   ✓   ✓

The controversy over policy towards China which has now lasted nearly eight years, has centered around three main questions. Should the People's Government in Peking be diplomatically recognized? Should it occupy the Chinese seat in the United Nations? And what should be the trading and cultural relations between Communist China and the Western world?

The arguments used on both sides have, naturally enough, changed somewhat as the years have gone by. The dispute began before the outbreak of the Korean War, but was then widely expected to be settled within a matter of months. Chinese intervention in Korea, while it left the basic attitudes of both sides unaltered, led to the whole quesion being put into cold storage until the fight-

[12] *Western World,* September, 1957, pp. 30-34. Reprinted by permission of the author.

ing was over. Since then, anxieties about Formosa, or the offshore islands or Indo-China have from time to time focused world opinion upon the issue, but have brought it, apparently, no nearer solution. The mere fact that everyone has become used to living with the problem has tended somewhat to reduce its explosive power. Nevertheless it remains important, as much on account of the embarrassments it causes between allies as for its effect upon relations between the West and the communist powers.

Through all vicissitudes two things have remained constant. The first is that the attitude of the United States has determined that of most of the governments—more than fifty of them—which do not recognize Peking. No one doubts that a change of American policy would reverse the present anti-Peking majority overnight. The second is that throughout the controversy, before and after the Korean fighting, as well as during it, United States government spokesmen have justified their policy in terms appropriate to a state of war.

Communist China, they say, is bent on world domination. It is an aggressor and morally and politically unfit to be a member of the United Nations. There is no point, they assert, in having cultural relations, let alone diplomatic ones, with such a pariah while any form of trade with it can only have the effect of strengthening a government which must be regarded as an enemy.

Normally one would expect to be at war with a country of which one spoke in such terms; and the United States is, in effect, at war with Communist China in every respect except the one usually regarded as most characteristic of a state of war—it is not fighting China by force of arms. . . .

Quite apart . . . from the question whether it is wise for the West to base its own world policy upon a doctrine of inevitable conflict, which it attributes to and condemns in the communist powers, and American application of the doctrine to China is cruder and less discriminating than that which the communists adopt towards the West, or than the Americans themselves adopt towards the Soviet Union and other communist countries. The communists appreciate, for instance, that if one intends to pursue a policy of implacable hostility throughout a prolonged period of so-called peace, one must be flexible in one's methods. To behave as one would in war, by cutting diplomatic relations, and by forbidding one's citizens to communicate or trade with other countries, at a time when military force is neither in use nor immediately in prospect, is to deprive oneself of the means of waging peace without securing the advantages of waging war.

This is just the unhappy state of frustrated impotence to which the United States has condemned itself in China in recent years. It has avoided this in its dealings with the Soviet Union. . . .

Dulles has recently replied to the obvious query as to why the United States does not treat the Soviet Union as it treats China, by saying that the United States would not have recognized the Soviet government in 1933 if it had then known how the Soviet Union would subsequently behave. Does anyone, however, really think that if the United States had refused all contact with the Soviet Union over the years, this would have advanced the cause of peace? Surely not; and surely this is why Dulles does not choose to break off relations now. Indeed now, when he knows very well how the Soviet Union behaves, he not only maintains diplomatic relations but permits Americans to visit the Soviet Union. . . . At the same time, however, he refuses Mrs. Roosevelt permission to visit China as a journalist.

These striking discrepancies are explicable only in terms of the psychology of certain sections of American opinion, not in terms of objective differences between the Soviet and Chinese communist situations.

Closely linked with diplomatic recognition is the question of China's representation in the United Nations. China is, under the Charter, a member of the organization and a permanent member of the Security Council. The United States, when asked why, in these circumstances, it will not contemplate China being represented in the United Nations by the government which has controlled China for eight years, gives two replies. The first, heard more faintly every year, is that the Peking government's grip on China may be broken at any minute. No one, however, believes this. It is strictly for the record. The second reply is that the Chinese government's behavior unfits it for membership in the world club. . . .

"The United Nations," Dulles magisterially stated the other day, "is not a reformatory for bad governments." Maybe not; but neither is it a Sunday school for good governments. Indeed its main role is not that of a school at all, but of a meeting place where international quarrels may be settled. If the United States is to do its job of settling disputes without war, those governments, wicked or virtuous, which are at loggerheads, must be able to meet there. The more they disapprove of each other, the more important it is that their confrontation should take place within the organization. Otherwise they may confront one another on the battlefield. The United Nations exists precisely to prevent this from happening.

By excluding the Peking government, which wields effective power in its country, one damages not Peking but the United Nations, which is thereby ruled out as an effective instrument of international conciliation. . . .

The question of trade relations, which has recently entered a new phase, with Britain leading a breakaway from the United States embargo, has damaged interallied cooperation more than it has held up Chinese development. Just defensible while fighting continued in Korea, the discrimination between the Soviet Union and China in this field ceased to make any sense several years ago. . . . What has caused the ill-feeling among allies is not the scale of the fortunes which businessmen felt they were losing, but the attitude towards the problem of world communism of which the American embargo is a symptom. The American policy could claim to offer useful results only on the assumption that a trial by war is going to occur within a few years; or that the major communist governments can be overturned by external action to prevent a rise in living standards of their peoples. Neither of these propositions is accepted by America's allies, still less can support for them be found among China's Asian neighbors. . . .

Supporters of American policy are entitled to ask what dividends have resulted from recognition of the Peking government, and what could be expected from a switch by the United States or from the admission of the Communist China to the United Nations.

It is true that Britain cannot point to striking benefits

to its interests in China, where British business has not been notably better treated than American. Nor have the Chinese ever been willing to exchange ambassadors with Britain.

To some extent this is due to Chinese resentment of the close relations which Britain has with the openly hostile United States. . . .

Other countries, both Asian and European, which have recognized Peking, but are uncommitted to any American alliance have certainly escaped some of Britain's disadvantages.

Moreover some of the benefits, which might have resulted from worldwide recognition of the People's government in 1950, were automatically ruled out when the United States succeeded in excluding it from the United Nations. Britain's policy not having been made effective, one could hardly expect to enjoy the fruits.

This reflection applies even more obviously to the hope which used to be expressed, that Chinese communists, if gently humored, would avoid close alignment with the Soviet Union and might even "go Titoist." This was probably always an over-optimistic forecast, though we are already seeing that Chinese Marxism can show independence of Moscow. Nevertheless, American policy since 1949 has undoubtedly cemented the Sino-Soviet alliance. A policy which draws one's supposed adversaries together is not on the face of it an intelligent one to follow and requires strong compensating advantages to justify it. In this case they are not easy to find.

To ask what can now be gained by a change is, perhaps, to pose the question wrongly. No one believes that admission to the United Nations or the general normalization of relations would transform Peking overnight into a cooperative regime. Experience with the Soviet Union, which is generally recognized, suggests no such thing. What is more pertinent is to ask what dangers and disadvantages might be avoided.

One has only to go back to the Geneva Conference on Indo-China in 1954 in order to see the inconvenience and even danger which arises when major powers will not speak to one another. . . . This was the lowest point of American postwar diplomatic prestige, and it was due directly to the anomalies inherent in the American attitude to China. It is very important that, if further crises involving China should arise, this tragi-comedy should not have to be repeated.

Quite as important is the effect of United States policies upon the rest of Asia. The United States has, of course, sufficient power to be able to buy the acquiescence of a few Asian states who need its military protection, but it is broadly true to say that no one in Asia except Syngman Rhee and Chiang Kai-shek comes anywhere near to sharing the American attitude to Peking.

For Asian countries, it is self-evident that they must seek coexistence with the communist regime in China. China to them looms larger than Russia and seems a much more permanent factor in the Asian scene than the United States. They do not believe that Chiang Kai-shek's government will ever see China again, nor do they expect the collapse of the mainland regime. The shifts and changes in personnel and policy, which have lately characterized both Moscow and Peking, lead very few Asians to draw the conclusion Dulles seems to draw—that continued external pressure may still overturn communism in China in favor of some more Jeffersonian conception. On the contrary, pressure of the American kind forces Chinese nationalism into alliance with the Communist Party inside China, while in the rest of Asia it helps to turn the spirit of Bandung into something specifically anti-Western.

In all this the United States shows itself surprisingly indifferent to the reactions of the uncommitted countries of Asia whose development and relationship with the new China are likely to determine the shape which Asia will take a generation hence. In particular it is curious that Americans, who have been more closely associated than any other Westerners with the postwar problems of Japan, should apparently make so little allowance for its future place on the Asian firmament.

To be simply a part of America's strategic "island chain," the outer perimeter of California's defenses, facing an ever-developing Sino-Soviet communist mainland, with whom it is expected to have the minimum of relations— this is surely a prospect which the rising generation of Japanese cannot be expected to accept. It is a restriction upon its economic means of livelihood and an attempt to deny its Asian character. . . .

No one, of course, is asking that the United States should abandon forthwith its painfully acquired positions of strength in the Far East, let alone that it should now contemplate the turning over of Formosa to communist rule. All that is asked is that an attempt should be made to look at the problem of the Far East in the long perspective of Asian development rather than in the short perspective of American strategy.

The interest of the United States in this area is not strikingly different from that of its allies. It is much less a question of the defense of the American continent and much more a question of laying foundations for the co-existence of China and its Asian neighbors than some American strategists can bring themselves to admit.

The interest of America's allies is the same—to find a new equilibrium which minimizes the danger of armed conflict, especially among the great powers, and leaves room for the upsurge of the new revolutionary forces which are so evident on both sides of the Iron Curtain in Asia. . . . These requirements are scarcely met at all by the attitude to China which has so far been dominant in the United States.

From the point of view of mutual confidence within the Western alliance, there is one further urgent need. It is to demonstrate that the United States is now framing its policies in the Far East, as it is already doing in other areas, upon the basis of an honest appraisal of world events and not upon the basis of prejudices deriving from its own domestic situation and its isolationist past.

To base the policy of great nations upon make-believe leads inevitably to deceiving of allies—as the Nationalists in Formosa were deceived about United States backing for a return to the mainland. It leads to the striking of fine attitudes followed by last minute withdrawals—as in the unfulfilled threats of all-out war in Korea or of nuclear intervention after Dien Bien Phu. When the moment of decision arrives, it is the realities which are added up and form the basis of action, but the resulting disillusionment can do a lot of damage.

Worst of all, prolonged dissemination of romantic myths ends by creating a public opinion, rooted in un-reality, which itself becomes a stubborn obstacle to statesmanship.

A SELECTED BIBLIOGRAPHY

ACHESON, DEAN G., *Power and Diplomacy*, Cambridge, Mass., 1958.
——, "The Illusion of Disengagement," *Foreign Affairs*, April, 1958.
AGAR, HERBERT, *The Price of Power*, Chicago, 1957.
BEAL, JOHN ROBINSON, *John Foster Dulles: A Biography*, New York, 1957.
BRODIE, BERNARD, *Strategy in the Missile Age*, Princeton, 1959.
CAMPBELL, JOHN C., *Defense in the Middle East*, New York, 1960.
DEUTCHER, ISAAC, *The Great Contest: Russia and the West*, New York, 1960.
EPSTEIN, LEON D., *Britain—Uncertain Ally*, Chicago, 1954.
FEIS, HERBERT, *The China Tangle*, Princeton, 1953.
——, *Between War and Peace: The Potsdam Conference*, Princeton, 1960.
FENNO, RICHARD F., JR. (ed.), *The Yalta Conference*, Boston, 1954.
FINLETTER, THOMAS K., *Power and Policy*, New York, 1954.
——, *Foreign Policy: The Next Phase*, New York, 1958.
FURNISS, EDGAR S., *France, Troubled Ally*, New York, 1960.
GRAEBNER, NORMAN A., *The New Isolationism*, New York, 1956.
HIGGINS, TRUMBULL, *Korea and the Fall of MacArthur*, New York, 1960.
JONES, JOSEPH, *The Fifteen Weeks*, New York, 1955.
KENNAN, GEORGE F., *American Diplomacy 1900-1950*, Chicago, 1951.
——, *Realities of American Foreign Policy*, Princeton, 1954.
——, *Russia, the Atom, and the West*, New York, 1957.
KISSINGER, HENRY A., *Nuclear Weapons and Foreign Policy*, New York, 1957.
KNORR, KLAUS (ed.), *NATO and American Security*, Princeton, 1959.
MARSHALL, CHARLES B., *Limits of Foreign Policy*, New York, 1954.

MORGENTHAU, HANS J., *In Defense of the National Interest,* New York, 1951.

MOSELY, PHILIP E., *The Kremlin and World Politics,* New York, 1960.

OSGOOD, ROBERT E., *Limited War,* Chicago, 1957.

PATTERSON, GARDNER and FURNISS, EDGAR S., JR., *NATO: A Critical Appraisal,* Princeton, 1957.

PAUKER, GUY J., "Southeast Asia as a Problem Area in the Next Decade," *World Politics,* April, 1959.

PEARSON, LESTER B., *Diplomacy in the Nuclear Age,* Cambridge, Mass., 1959.

REISCHAUER, EDWIN O., *Wanted: An Asian Policy,* New York, 1955.

REITZEL, WILLIAM *et al.,* *United States Foreign Policy 1945-1955,* Washington, 1956.

ROBERTS, HENRY L., *Russia and America: Dangers and Prospects,* New York, 1956.

SNELL, JOHN L. (ed.), *The Meaning of Yalta,* Baton Rouge, La., 1956.

SPANIER, JOHN W., *American Foreign Policy Since World War II,* New York, 1960.

STEVENSON, ADLAI E., *Call to Greatness,* New York, 1954.

SULZBERGER, C. L., *What's Wrong with U.S. Foreign Policy,* New York, 1959.

THOMPSON, KENNETH W., *Political Realism and the Crisis of World Politics,* Princeton, 1960.

WESTERFIELD, H. BRADFORD, *Foreign Policy and Party Politics, Pearl Harbor to Korea,* New Haven, 1955.

INDEX

190

VAN NOSTRAND ANVIL BOOKS already published